BASEBALL DADS

THE GAME'S GREATEST PLAYERS REFLECT ON
THEIR FATHERS AND THE GAME THEY LOVE

BASEBALL DADS

WAYNE STEWART

Skyhorse Publishing

Skyhorse Publishing books may be purchased in bulk at special discounts for sales promotion, corporate gifts, fund-raising, or educational purposes. Special editions can also be created to specifications. For details, contact the Special Sales Department, Skyhorse Publishing, 307 West 36th Street, 11th Floor, New York, NY 10018 or info@skyhorsepublishing.com.

Skyhorse® and Skyhorse Publishing® are registered trademarks of Skyhorse Publishing, Inc. ®, a Delaware corporation.

www.skyhorsepublishing.com

10 9 8 7 6 5 4 3 2 1

Library of Congress Cataloging-in-Publication Data

Stewart, Wayne, 1951-
 Baseball dads : the game's greatest players reflect on their fathers and the game they love / Wayne Stewart.
    p. cm.
 ISBN 978-1-61608-583-4 (hardcover : alk. paper)
 1. Baseball players--United States--Biography. 2. Fathers and sons--United States.
 3. Baseball--United States. I. Title.
 GV865.A1.S799 2112
 796.3570922--dc23
 [B]

2012002371

Printed in the United States of America

For a book on the love between fathers and sons, the only
possible dedication has to be: To my father,
Owen J. Stewart (he was known by everyone as O. J. long
before the infamy attached to those initials). Also, again
quite naturally given the nature of this book, I dedicate this
book to my two sons Sean and Scott, and to Sean's son,
my wonderful grandson Nathan Stewart.

Contents

Acknowledgments

First, a big thank you goes out to the players who gave up their time, allowing me to interview them and to delve into their relationships with their fathers. My appreciation also goes out to the always-helpful Susie Giuliano of the Cleveland Indians communications department; Leah Tobin of the Boston Red Sox media department; and Mark Langill of the Los Angeles Dodgers. Thanks also to my editor Mark Weinstein for his enormous guidance on this book and throughout many years.

BASEBALL DADS

Reflections on Fathers and Sons

In 2002 when I wrote *Fathers, Sons, and Baseball*, a book about the love between fathers and sons and their link with baseball, the first thought that sprang into my mind was a basketball story, not a baseball one. It was one which vividly portrays the way a devoted father feels about his son. Legendary coach Al McGuire, who won the national title at Marquette, once coached his son Allie. In his sophomore season Allie and George Frazier were competing against each other for playing time. Frazier felt he should have been getting more action than Allie, and told his coach as much. Candidly, McGuire told him, "George, I love my son. For you to play, you have to be twice as good as him."

While one focus of *Baseball Dads* is baseball, by far the more important topic herein is the relationship between father and son. From the families that have produced three-generations of major league players to the father who spends hours playing catch with a son—who possesses little talent and absolutely no chance of making it to the major leagues yet loves the game—the warmth, pride, love, and even tenderness which spreads throughout families, handed down from father to son endures. The sharing of the love of baseball between a father and his son permeates this book like the aroma of sizzling bacon on a Sunday morning, wafting up to and awakening a sleeping boy. Baseball—the most succulent and nurturing sport of all for a dad and his son —has been, and remains, a marvelous bonding experience.

This book touches on just a few former big league ballplayers whose sons also played in the majors; these relationships are often both complex and fascinating.

In my previous book the ramifications, both positive and negative, of being the offspring of a big leaguer were covered. One aspect of this unique relationship is the inherent risk of the son being overshadowed by the father. However, even when this happens to men such as Stan Musial, whose son Dick ran track at Notre Dame but never really got into baseball, they try to protect their sons and assuage any doubts or insecurities their offspring may have developed from being compared to their fathers. In fact, Stan once said that in some ways he was happy his son was not interested in baseball—he wanted what he knew to be best for Dick, and it wasn't a lifetime of baseball.

Clearly, for many it is not easy being the son of a superstar. In addition, if one's surname is unusual, unmistakable (e.g. Yastrzemski), or if a young player lugs around a name with a "Junior" attached to it (think, for example, Pete Rose, Jr. or Tony Gwynn, Jr.), there's no hiding from who you are or the pressure to match your dad's legacy.

Then there are the fan's inevitably high expectations and their sometimes unfair pre-judgments to cope with. As Cal Ripken, Jr. said when his son Ryan was selected to play in the 2011 Under Armour©All-American Baseball Game, "There are some positives associated with that [bearing the name Ripken], but in many ways there's a burden that comes with the last name. I think a lot of people sort of expect a lot out of him." Critics often are intolerant of the mistakes and the normal failures of sons of famous players. Ripken, Sr., by the way, is one of six men to manage his son in the majors, and the only one to manage two of his sons (Billy and Cal with the Orioles).

Mike Yastrzemski, Carl's son, said, "I just have to deal with it. . . . I'm not concerned with trying to impress somebody else. All I'm concerned about is proving to myself that I can play." One of his minor league managers cautioned, "Don't try to compare him to his father. That wouldn't be fair to him." Unfortunately, comparisons   inevitably follow. Mike, who said his father was "always there to talk baseball with," made an All-Star team when he was with the Birmingham Barons, but never made it to the "Show."

In the June Amateur Draft of 2009 the Boston Red Sox drafted a high school outfielder, yet another Yastrzemski: Carl's grandson Michael. He went late, in the thirty-sixth round on the final day of the draft, but Boston fans couldn't help but smile when they heard about the selection.

Baseball can be a cold business, but sometimes it shows a compassionate face. In June of 2002, the Red Sox signed thirty-three-year-old John Henry Williams, the son of the man who roamed left field just prior to Yaz, Ted Williams. The contract his son signed was one which placed him on a Red Sox rookie team in the Gulf Coast League. The move certainly seemed like it was all just a goodwill gesture (with Ted orchestrating things for his son just a few weeks prior to his demise) because John had never played pro ball before. The media gave John Henry the nickname "The Kid's Kid." One Boston official admitted the signing was "unusual," but said that due to the prestige of Ted, the Red Sox had been "willing to go beyond the norm." Needless to say, John—unlike his father—was not cut out to be a major league, or for that matter, a minor league hitter. By August he was through; he announced he was quitting, giving up his dream of forging a career in baseball.

In the June 2010 baseball draft, three sons of the big league managers Jim Leyland, Bruce Bochy, and Ozzie Guillen, were selected by the team their fathers ran. Call it goodwill gestures, nepotism, or a sort of sage insider "trading," but Leyland, for one, defended the selection of his son Patrick who, like Jim, was a catcher.

Interestingly, before Leyland had been lured out of retirement to manage the Detroit Tigers in 2006 he had been courted by several other teams that had dangled millions of dollars in front of him. He rejected all of the tantalizing offers only to accept an offer to coach a team for free.

That team was a youth league team in Western Pennsylvania's Beaver County. The catch? He would be able to guide the team his eleven-year-old son was on — that son being the aforementioned Patrick. So, passing up money and fame to coach your son? That's what love does to us.

Then fifty-eight years old, and with a World Series title to his credit, Leyland enthusiastically worked with the youngsters but admitted that like any father, he was nervous watching his son. According to AP sports writer Alan Robinson, Leyland felt just as "edgy watching his team play as he was in the majors."

Tim "Rock" Raines, Sr. always wanted to duplicate what the Griffeys had done and play in the same big league game with his son — "Rock" and his son had once played against each other in a minor league contest and another time in a spring training affair. "Rock" was forced to retire when he developed lupus in 1999, putting a crimp on his father-son plans. He came out of retirement in 2001 though, and proved that his revival was no fluke—he hit .308 for the Montreal Expos. That set the stage for his dream game with Tim, Jr.

The younger Raines, "Little Rock," said one of his fondest baseball memories was when he played in a father-son game held by his father's Montreal Expos when he was about seven years old. "I remember getting all dressed up in a uniform with my dad's number and my name on the back." In early October of 2001, he had worked his way up to the majors with the Orioles and he learned that the Expos, in a sentimental and considerate gesture, had just sent his father to Baltimore in a trade from which they received virtually nothing in return. On October 3 they both got into a game against the Red Sox although Junior was employed only as a pinch hitter. Then the following day the Raines duo made up two-thirds of Baltimore's outfield, with the "old man" in left field and his son beside him in center. It was a day to cherish forever.

More recently, Howard Johnson came out of retirement in 2011 at the age of fifty to play in two independent league games with his son Glen. In his first contest Howard went 0-for-4 for the Rockland Boulders, who had signed both Howard and Glen in September to set up the special father-son situation. "Hojo" drew a walk in the second game before moving over to the first base coach's box; he was through as a player, but satisfied as a father. He commented that his biggest thrill "was standing on deck while I watched my son in the batter's box. At that moment, I have never felt closer to him or been more proud of who he has become."

Coincidentally, the team that the father/son Johnson and Johnson duo faced featured Tim Raines as their manager with his son as a player.

Naturally, with today's athletes getting bigger and better than ever before—and with today's high tech training methods, medical improvements, and better equipment—many sons exceed their fathers' accomplishments on the baseball fields. As good as Ken Griffey, Sr. was—and make no mistake, his .296 lifetime batting average and his selection to three All-Star teams serve as proof he *was* good—his son still shot by him. Junior's 630 lifetime home runs, fifth most all-time, and his ten Gold Gloves are overwhelming accomplishments.

Robinson Canó likewise, is a much better second baseman than his father José was a big league pitcher. José pitched in just six big league games during a brief stint with Houston. The last time he threw off a big league mound was late in 1989. In all, he went 1-1 with a 5.09 ERA; and even though his final appearance was a complete game victory, his career was over—the classic tale of a guy getting only a quick cup of major league "coffee." In the meantime, Robinson was a career .308 hitter through 2011. Regardless, their baseball bond was vividly on display during the 2011 Home Run Derby, an event held each season as part of the All-Star Game festivities.

For the first time ever, according to a report from the MLB network, a Derby participant chose his father to feed him a steady diet of juicy pitch after juicy pitch. José a trim and fit forty-nine-year-old, knew just where to serve up his pitches. Robinson, like his father, was a native of San Pedro de Macorís in the Dominican Republic, a hotbed for baseball talent. He hit homers with the frequency of lightning bug sightings on those summer nights when fireflies blink out their Morse code mating signals again and again. Both Canós wore a jersey adorned by the same number, 24, Robinson's normal uniform number. Robinson stepped into the batter's box and tattooed the ball, depositing thirty-two of dad's pitches into the stands over three rounds. That included a new record of a dozen homers in the final round.

When Robinson hit a home run to draw into a tie in the final round, he took a time-out to hug his father—who throws to Robinson often in the offseason—and to tell him he loved him.

After swatting the Derby-winning homer, Robinson dashed up to his father and took a joyful leap into his arms. José supported him in a scene vaguely reminiscent of the time Yogi Berra jumped into the arms of Don Larsen after the two worked together on crafting the only perfect game in World Series history. No. Better yet, it was more like Robinson had, for just one magical moment, become the little boy once more, jumping up into daddy's embrace. Either way, it was a moment of elation, one that cried out, "We did it!"

There are myriad remarkable and interesting stories involving baseball families. It's not exactly rare for a father to produce two or more sons who were talented enough to make it to the majors—Cal Ripken, Sr. with sons Cal, Jr. and Billy come quickly to mind. One father even had two sons, Harry and Dixie Walker, who both went on to win batting titles. Another father had *five* sons who all played in the big leagues: the Delahanty crew. There have even been cases of twin brothers playing in the pros (e.g. Jose and Ozzie Canseco and Eddie and Johnny O'Brien).

Dave and Gail Weaver have a lot to be proud of, having produced two sons, Jeff and Jered, who made it to the majors. Jered has enjoyed a better career than Jeff, but nobody can take away the fact that both Weaver boys reached the apex of their field. As a rookie in 2006, Jered would cruise to an 11-2 record. He even fired seven innings of shutout ball in his big league debut with his older brother and fellow member of the Angels starting staff (for the moment, at least) watching from the Angel's dugout. That season Jered won his first nine decisions, nearly becoming just the third pitcher to win his first ten as a starter.

Interestingly and lamentably for the Weaver family, by June 30, 2006, Jeff's stats were deteriorating, and with an albatross-like salary of $8,325,000, the Angels, according to wire reports, "swapped one Weaver brother for another, designating right-hander Jeff for assignment and replacing him" on the roster with Jered who earned $385,000.

Jeff wound up making it to the playoffs with the Cardinals at season's end. Jered, who had dedicated his fifth straight win earlier that year to Jeff, announced he would attend each of his brother's postseason games, to support him and to spend time with him.

From his auspicious beginnings Jered led his league in strikeouts in 2010; and through 2011, he holds a laudatory lifetime .636 win-loss percentage.

One game, though, remains as perhaps the most memorable contest ever to the Weaver family: the time Jered and Jeff started against each other back on June 20, 2009. The contest marked the twenty-first time brothers opposed each other in the majors.

Los Angeles took a 6-4 decision with Jeff winning. Jered, hit hard, absorbed the loss. Dodgers' manager Joe Torre said it was appropriate for his pitcher to win: "The older one should have won."

Jeff admitted it had been "one of the most ill-felt victories ever, but you take wins whenever you can get them. I'm glad it's all said and done. . . . You always wish the best for him. . . ."

Jered said that facing his brother had been fun but he hoped the brotherly duel never again materialized—it didn't. He said it "was draining enough having to do it one time. . . . I'm glad it's over with." Clearly his father related to his sons' sentiments.

Gail said, "It was very emotional. It is not a comfortable feeling; you want them both to do well because they are doing the best that they can and we are just rooting for both of them."

Gail and Dave—who lowered his head each time one of his boys surrendered a run—sat behind the plate, about twenty rows up, wearing, reported the AP, "half Angels/half Dodgers jerseys that appeared to be stitched together in the back." Because both sons wore jersey number 36, picking a number for their homemade uniforms was no issue.

In 2002 when Charles Benes watched his two sons Andy and Alan square off, the proud papa sat in a box seat halfway between the dugouts and switched off between wearing Cubs and Cardinals caps each half inning.

While this book will mainly cover major league players whose fathers did not play baseball for a living, there are many families in which—due the powerful lure of baseball—both father and son had jobs *related* to baseball. Several families produced baseball announcers including the three-generation Carays—Harry, Skip, and Chip. And José Mota, son of ex-big leaguer Manny, started out as a marginal ballplayer then became a bi-lingual broadcaster who uses both English and Spanish on the air.

There have also been families with three generations of umpires— the Runges are represented by Ed, Paul, and Brian. Additionally, Shag Crawford, who umpired more than 3,000 games, had a son Jerry who also umped in the majors and another son, Joey, who became an NBA official. Bill Haller once worked the plate in a game in which his brother Tom caught—imagine a father's trepidation watching that game. Years later Tom joked about his situation: "When you have a brother who's an umpire and you're still only hitting .200, it's time to get out." Rules now prohibit umpires from working the plate during games in which a relative is playing.

Then there were the Newhans, who have the unusual distinction of having a father who gained more baseball glory without ever once picking up a bat, than his son who played in eight big league seasons. Ross, the father, is a sportswriter who was honored by baseball's Hall of Fame when he won the J. G. Taylor Spink Award in 2000, while David was a .253 hitter for five clubs. When his dad was officially inducted, Dave commented, "It is an honor to be recognized as his son."

There are also interesting cases in which one family member is famous in one field (quite often in a sport other than baseball) while the other made it to the major league level in baseball.

One such example is the Snow family. J. T. Snow was a standout first baseman who won six Gold Gloves for his fielding prowess. Meanwhile, his father Jack also possessed a fine pair of hands and snared forty-five touchdown passes over his 150 contests played in the NFL.

In 2011 the son of hockey Hall of Famer Wayne Gretzky, Trevor, signed a contract with the Cubs who were impressed by his hitting skills, which he had displayed as a first baseman for Oaks Christian High School in California. He was also his football squad's quarterback and a teammate of the sons of Joe Montana and actor Will Smith.

Then there are families such as the McGraws and the Jacksons. Some might argue that Tug McGraw was not as famous in baseball as his son Tim is as a country western legend. Meanwhile Connor Jackson has an actor—John from the TV series *JAG*—for a father.

Many men who succeeded in baseball thanked their fathers for the life lessons they had imparted to them. One example: Sparky Anderson, a man Bob Costas described as "one of the nicest people I've ever encountered in sports." Anderson, said Costas, "never big-timed anybody" and gave his time freely to both famous members of the media and "a cub reporter from a suburban newspaper."

Anderson noted that such behavior came directly from his father: "My daddy said, 'I'm going to give you a gift and if you live with it everything will work perfect and it won't cost you a dime. Every day of your life and every person that you meet, you will just be nice to that person and treat that person like they are someone.'"

Jim Thome showed his thanks for all his father Chuck had taught him with a special gift after he had drilled his 500th homer. He drove him to Cooperstown, New York, to present the souvenir baseball to the Hall of Fame. He told *Sports Illustrated:* that visit "was one of the greatest days of my dad's life."

Jim said that the best advice about baseball he ever heard came from Chuck who told him, "Don't believe the hype." Those simple but sage words helped Jim stayed grounded throughout his career. He also said that one of the main reasons he never took performance-enhancing drugs was because if he had, he would never again have been able to look his father in the eye.

Like Thome, baseball teams appreciate dads, too. In a 2011 ceremony to celebrate Derek Jeter's 3,000th hit, the Yankees gave both Jeter and his father rings, each adorned with fifty diamonds, to commemorate his achievement.

Teammates also respect fatherhood. On the evening of August 4, 2011, the Indians were in Boston when Jack Hannahan was informed that his wife Jenny was in labor with their first child even though she wasn't due until late October. Hannahan discovered the earliest flight back home would be the next morning so he looked into booking a private jet. However, the price tag for such a ride was as steep as a plane's ascension upon takeoff and Hannahan was earning just $500,000. "I can't afford to drop forty or fifty grand on a flight," said Hannahan. Teammates, aware of his plight, told Cleveland's traveling secretary to go ahead and book the trip for him—they would pick up the tab (which reportedly wound up at $35,000).

The Indians, Travis Hafner aside, were not a team comprised of big-ticket players, but that didn't matter. Teammate Justin Masterson, a leading organizer of the chipping-money-in campaign, stated, "Everybody on this team, young and old, put something together to help Hannie out," and he added that the prevailing feeling was, "He needs to be there." They were, as Indians manager Manny Acta pointed out, "so unselfish . . . that's what is going to make this special for years to come."

Hannahan arrived at the hospital fifteen minutes before his son John—checking in at just two pounds, twelve ounces—was born after an emergency cesarean procedure. "He's our little miracle," smiled the new father. Upon returning to the lineup Hannahan, normally a light hitter, went on a .420 tear lasting into September.

When the Louisville Slugger people heard the story, they shipped a regulation bat with the baby's name, birth weight, and birthday carved into the barrel.

Quite often a ballplayer's son will unequivocally state that his father is his favorite big leaguer (e.g. Ken Griffey, Jr.). Not always. Paul Byrd, a winner of 109 games over his fourteen seasons in the majors, recalled the time the younger of his two sons, Colby, saw him signing autographs for fans. Byrd related how his son was puzzled: "I was signing . . . and he says, 'What do they want your autograph for? You're average!' And, 'Oh, I thought if you were good you'd be on the Yankees.'"

Then in 2005—when Paul brought his wife Kym, Colby, and his other son Grayson to Yankee Stadium to see him work the third game of the American League Division Series against New York's ace, Randy Johnson—Paul thought Colby would finally be impressed. He wasn't—he wanted to return to the hotel room so he could play Nintendo. Paul joked, "I was like, 'What's a guy gotta' do for you to be proud of your dad?' I'm the Rodney Dangerfield of parents." Of course many children of big leaguers—at least when they get old enough—do, in fact, appreciate what their fathers do for a living.

It also remains true, though that no matter what, quite often a man is not a king in his own home. As far as the world of baseball goes, no matter how big a star a player is or how proud his kids may be of him, the father frequently remains "just dad." On the plus side of that ledger, even if a player comes home after an 0-for-5 day at the plate, he will be loved just the same by his child/children—he's still just good old dad and the child never loses that unconditional love.

Sometimes a son will realize his father's wisdom is always at his disposal and he appreciates hearing advice on baseball. Although these lessons don't always come easily or quickly. Dusty Baker once confessed that he regretted not listening to his father's advice. During the 1981 NLCS, Baker got into a skirmish with an Expos fan in Montreal and hurt his hand. The first person Baker turned to was his father. "I called my dad. My dad was like, 'I told you, boy, about being so wild.'" Dusty was able to continue to play as his Los Angeles Dodgers advanced to the World Series, but, impaired, he hit just .167 (4-for-24) and he struck out on six of those at bats. Twenty-one years later Baker still remembered the incident, saying, "That's probably my ghost, when you've been told something all your life by your father, then you end up doing exactly what he told you not to do." Even huge stars have those I-shoulda'-listened-to-dad moments; and even dads of big leaguers can't resist reverting back to their days as patriarchs issuing their I-told-you-so's.

Darin Erstad *did* listen to his father, and the words he heard stuck with him for a lifetime. When the Anaheim Angels won the World Series in 2002, the last pitch was lofted off the bat of San Francisco's Kenny Lofton and into Erstad's center field territory. He told *Sports Illustrated* that while he was initially aware of the deafening roar of the throng on hand that day, he suddenly tuned out the crowd. He did, though, hear a voice in his mind: that of his father, Chuck. "It was not," reported the magazine, "coming from the stands where his father watched. It was coming from his childhood, far back to when his father taught him how to catch." The voice was reminding him to use two hands. Erstad would later comment, "That's what came to me. It had never happened before, but I heard him. It was pretty neat." The cliché of "father knows best" and the fatherly lesson of always adhering to the basics of baseball applied as Erstad made the catch and secured the world championship.

In addition to all the tales of advice, love, and happiness shared between fathers and sons, sadly, there are also tragedies involving many baseball fathers and sons. One painful example took place when Louis "Bobo" Newsom pitched for the Yankees in a 1947 game he would never forget. He had been toiling for the hapless Washington Senators when he received a mid-season reprieve, acquired on waivers by the Yankees who stormed their way into the World Series. After one of his two outings in that Series he was informed that his father, who was in attendance that day, had died of a heart attack while watching the game.

Some of the tragic stories are very touching ones. In 2004 Thurman Munson's son Michael proposed marriage to Michelle Bruey and wanted to do so in a way which would include his father who had passed away in an August 1979 plane crash. He escorted Michelle to Yankee Stadium on an Old-Timer's Day, took a knee, showed her an engagement ring, and popped the question. Trembling with emotion, she accepted. Thurman's widow, Diana, along with Michael, his two siblings, and five of Munson's grandchildren were on the field when Diana was given the honor of throwing out the ceremonial first pitch that day.

Jack Tarasco, the father of major league outfielder Tony, once requested his son scatter his ashes over the Pasadena field where Tony had begun his first days of playing baseball. Tony obliged not long after his seventy-four-year-old father's life was claimed by pneumonia in April of 2001. Tony, who was then playing for the Triple-A Norfolk Tides in the New York Mets minor league chain, thought ahead and saved some of his father's ashes. When the Mets called Tony up to the parent club in April of the following season he took those ashes to Shea Stadium and on April 11, the day after his first appearance with his new club, spread them close to the outfield fence. Later in the year when he made a circus catch near that location he stated, "My father's spirit has been with me since he passed."

Pitcher Brian Moehler also paid homage to his father Fred (who never had the opportunity to see Brian pitch in the big leagues), doing so each and every time he took to the mound in the majors. Just prior to his first pitch, Brian would write his late father's initials in the dirt of the mound. "It's just to remind me that without him, I wouldn't be where I am today."

When Robert Fick's father Charlie was battling cancer and undergoing chemotherapy, Robert naturally empathized with his dad who had lost his hair. In a touching, tender gesture, the Detroit Tigers All-Star had his head shaved.

Bernie Williams, whose real first name is Bernabe, also had to cope with a very sick father. On April 9, 2001, the New York Yankees, understanding the importance of family, permitted Williams to fly to Puerto Rico to be with his seventy-three-year-old father, Bernabe Williams, Sr., who for years had been suffering from pulmonary fibrosis.

At one point Bernie asked his father if he could travel back to New York and resume playing again. His father grasped his arm and clung to it. Bernie took that to mean Bernabe still needed him. Later Bernie did leave his father but only after his dad had pointed to his son then put his arms out in a gesture that resembled a child imitating an airplane in flight. "That's when I knew he was better and it was time to go," said Bernie.

The first day he was back with his team, April 20, he commented that "baseball is only a small part of my life when something that significant happens. All my thoughts and prayers and focus were on my father's situation." He said that he had followed the progress of his teammates through highlights and scores, "but all my thoughts were on my dad." His priorities were as clear as they were solid: baseball is great—it was, after all, his profession, and it even helped him bond with his father—but in the end, family comes first.

After Bernie returned to the Yankee lineup for a considerable stretch he denied being distracted by his father's condition, but he found himself mired in a 13-for-69 (.188) slump. Having missed eleven days to be with his father, he attributed his cold spell to rustiness but admitted, "It's not easy, that's for sure. It's not easy." Although he apparently didn't realize how close to death his father was, Bernie believed, as he told the press, that his father would probably be "going in and out of the hospital for the next year or so. That's the reality of his situation. Every day his lungs are getting less and less functional and eventually he will run out of air. It's a terrifying feeling."

The prognosis Bernie alluded to didn't pan out. Reality was much harsher—Bernabe died on May 13th in Bayamon, Puerto Rico, one day after Bernie had stated he expected his father would be released from the intensive care unit soon.

After hearing that his father had suffered a heart attack, Bernie once again took off to be at his side. This time he was too late. Sadly, Bernabe died about an hour before his son arrived at the hospital. Williams' manager, Joe Torre, noted, "It's a very traumatic time. He's had a lot to deal with. I don't think his dad would have known he was there, anyway. His system was pretty well shut down." Torre told his center fielder to take as much time as he needed to rejoin the Yankees.

Eventually, and remarkably, Bernie somehow shook off his woes and tribulations and hit .307, the same batting average he compiled the season before, with twenty-six home runs. His three homers and 10 RBI over ten games during the first two rounds of postseason play versus Oakland and Seattle helped thrust the Yankees into the World Series where they came up short against the Arizona Diamondbacks. Bernie had to be thinking his father was looking down on him, rooting him on every step of the way.

Then there was the loss of J. T. Snow's father Jack. In spring training of the 2006 season, just months after Jack died of a staph infection, J. T. reported to the Boston Red Sox camp requesting to wear jersey number 84. A veteran player wearing a jersey number that high is virtually unheard of, but J. T. knew what he was doing. His father had worn 84 when he was a receiver for the Los Angeles Rams back in the 1960s and into the 1970s after his tenure on the Notre Dame gridiron where he was an All-American.

Jack, who said he loved watching his son play when he was just a tyke because of his sheer enthusiasm for baseball, had always told his son to enjoy the sport and to play hard be it in a spring training game or a World Series contest. When his son did get to play in the 2002 World Series, Jack had advised, "Be a part of that and enjoy it because you may never come back down this road again." He didn't, but he did savor the words of his father and he has continued to cherish his father's memory forever.

John Franco—who, over his lengthy twenty-one-year career racked up a lofty 424 saves (number four all-time—trailing just Trevor Hoffman, Mariano Rivera, and Lee Smith)—could, like any pitcher, go through some tough times. He once commented, "I used to go to my dad at times like this, but can't any more." That is the lament shared by so many sons, especially those who lost their father when they were still young.

These sons feel as if they have been prematurely robbed of not only a loved one, but of a trusted person they could open up to, ask advice of, and in all ways rely upon. During a particularly rough spell in 1993, six years after his father's demise, John ended the season with a balloon-like ERA of 5.20. More than ever before, John needed the help of his father. A piece in the *New York Times* stated, "When he kicks the rosin bag, cranes his neck and seems to be searching for something in the sky, he is: his father."

During troubling days James would console John, "Heck with 'em. You can pitch." Earlier, when John considered dropping out of St. John's University, it was James who talked him out of what would have been a disastrous decision.

"[There] isn't a day that goes by that I don't think of him," he said of his father, a New York City sanitation worker. James passed away in October of 1987 due to a heart attack he suffered while sitting in his New York garbage truck. As a tribute to him, John wore an orange T-shirt every time he played which read Department of Sanitation, New York City and which had belonged to his dad. In addition, John took a pebble from his father's grave site and kept it inside his black travel kit. It went with him on road trips: a talisman. Another ritual he adhered to was polishing James' sanitation department badge. Forget his father? Never.

Growing up in the Bensonhurst section of Brooklyn, the Franco family lived very modestly, without much money to spare. As a kid John used to redeem twenty empty milk cartons for an upper deck seat in Shea Stadium to watch his favorite team, the very same team he would gain most of his fame with, the Mets. John was wealthy in other ways, with that intangible "wealth" being manifested strongly by the love of family. He was, without fail, encouraged by James in everything he endeavored. James even taught his son to throw an effective overhand curve.

John attended the same high school, Lafayette High in Brooklyn, that Sandy Koufax had attended. Even back then it was apparent John had talent, especially when he twirled two no-hitters during his freshman season at St. John's in Queens.

Many years later when John made it to his first and only World Series, as a member of the 2000 New York Mets, he ruminated once again about his dad. He said he was relishing the experience of being in the Series, "because I've played so long to get here," but naturally wished his father was there by his side. In a way, James was there. At one point fellow Mets pitcher Al Leiter asked John what he had been gazing at and he replied, "I'm looking at that brightest star—that's my papa." Leiter said, "That's probably my dad up there with him. They're probably having a beer and laughing at us."

In 2003 Baltimore Orioles catcher Brook Fordyce asked his manager, Mike Hargrove, if he could play in their team's game the day after his father had passed away. He would return home the following day for the funeral, but he insisted on playing because, as Hargrove recalled, "He said that's what his father would have wanted him to do."

Similarly, Yankee outfielder Paul O'Neill played the fourth game of the 1999 World Series shortly after his seventy-nine-year-old father Charles had passed away after a lengthy bout of heart problems about three hours after Game Three. O'Neill took an 0-for-3 and drew a walk as New York swept the Atlanta Braves to capture yet another World Series.

During the jubilant on-the-field celebration, O'Neill, openly sobbing, hugged his manager Joe Torre who told his mourning right fielder, "Your dad got to watch this one." In the clubhouse O'Neill tearfully spoke of how he was proud to be a member of the world champs, then added, "but believe me, I lost someone special." Teammate Roger Clemens observed, "I don't know if I could've done what Paul O'Neill did." Close friend Joe Girardi summed it up: "He understood that his father wanted him to go out there."

Years later during a TV interview O'Neill told Tim McCarver that somehow, even in the middle of a stadium jammed with 50,000 spectators, "You always knew where your father was. You got just as much satisfaction from watching him smile after a big game than you did for what you did yourself." It was as if, in a positive way, the son and not the father was enjoying a vicarious delight.

While separation from one's family is not as tragic as death, it can be a traumatic situation. Consider the case of Luis Tiant. Born in Marianao, Cuba, Tiant is the son of Luis, Sr. and Isabel. The senior Luis was a splendid southpaw pitcher who for two decades gained fame in the Cuban Leagues and the American Negro Leagues. Armed with an assortment of pitches, his style on the mound was a precursor to his son's—they both utilized "an exaggerated pirouette pitching motion." Senior continued to ply his trade into his forties and, as a forty-one-year-old, posted an unblemished 10-0 record during an All-Star season in 1947 with the New York Cubans.

Although Luis showed signs of becoming a promising pitcher as a teenager and shared a love of baseball with his father, Luis, Sr. discouraged his son from attempting to become a professional pitcher, doing so for one very logical reason. He was convinced that being black was enough to prevent his son from making a good living in the game.

However, Luis continued to pitch and pitch well, even though he would say many years later, "I am nowhere near the pitcher my father was." By 1959 he was in pro ball as an eighteen-year-old hurler with the Mexico City Tigers. He remained with them for three seasons, returning to Cuba during offseasons to play winter ball in front of family and friends.

Around this time Cuba's leader Fidel Castro decided that due to the political embarrassment and potential economic hardship of massive Cuban emigration he would forbid Cuban citizens from leaving the island.

Foreseeing a difficult situation, Luis, Sr. told his son not to come home after his 1961 season in Mexico.

It was around this time that newlywed Luis experienced another life changing event when he became the property of the Cleveland Indians. He spent 1962 and 1963 in their farm system and then debuted with the Indians in 1964. He would stay in the majors for nineteen seasons.

By 1975 his yearning to be reunited with his parents grew deeper than ever. Now an established, though aging, star player with the Boston Red Sox, Tiant had seen his mother just once since his decision not to return to Cuba. This visit with her had taken place in 1968 when his father was, according to reports, placed in jail as a way of guaranteeing his wife would not defect. Now Tiant wanted to see both parents once more, especially because it had been fourteen years since he laid eyes on his father .

In May of 1975 good fortune came Luis' way. United States Senator George McGovern visited Castro and gave him a letter from another Senator, Edward Brooke III of Massachusetts, requesting that Castro allow Luis' parents to visit him in Boston. Castro, a huge baseball fan, relented and on August 21, 1975, Isabel and Luis arrived at Logan Airport in Boston where they were met by their famous son. Luis hugged his father "and shamelessly wept." Isabel turned to her son and said, "I'm so happy I don't care if I die now."

Five days later Luis, Sr., accompanied by his son, threw out the ceremonial first pitch for a game his son was starting. Actually, he threw *two* "first" pitches. Displeased with his first toss, a fastball thrown low and out of the strike zone from a full windup, he asked Red Sox catcher Tim Blackwell for the ball and made another throw — this one a knuckler which butterflied its way across home plate. Luis later revealed that after the second pitch his father had told him on the mound that "he was ready to go four or five [innings]."

After a shaky start that night and another in his next outing, Luis caught fire and helped lead the Red Sox into postseason play. His eighteen victories helped guide Boston to the World Series only to lose there to the Cincinnati Reds, but it had been quite a ride for father and son, and the following season, with family in the stands, he won twenty-one games while dropping only twelve decisions.

Wisely, his parents never returned to Cuba, staying with their son for fifteen months until Luis, Sr. passed away in December of 1976. Then, just two days after his death, Isabel sat in a chair to rest before attending her husband's memorial service. She never got up. The couple was buried next to each other not far from their son's Milton, Massachusetts home.

The bond between father and son is the basis for many such interesting and compelling tales, and within this book we'll explore this special relationship further by profiling a cast of fascinating fathers and sons in more depth. Many of these father and son duos are bona fide big league superstars; some of them have fathers who played in the majors; and others were raised by fathers with more humble beginnings. All of this, however, is immaterial because the prevailing, universal theme and the primary purpose of this book is to revel in the joy and beauty of the love between father and son. It's through these stories that one is able to see how the love of baseball has brought so many fathers and sons together.

It's as if every day of the baseball season is Father's Day. Certainly, all of the hours that were whiled away languorously in games of catch, of playing Wiffle ball, of engaging in fantasy baseball, and of compiling baseball card collections, were well spent. The bystander-thrills and the excitement that comes with seeing a son play on a baseball field, whether it's a dirt sandlot, a local Little League surface, or a well-manicured big league diamond, are priceless and remain unforgettable. The memories become as entrenched in a father's memory as his first glimpse of his son in his hospital's maternity ward.

This book contains the stories of love, devotion, diligence, and sacrifice of fifteen families. These qualities and emotions are as palpable as they are everlasting.

Joba Chamberlain

Photo Courtesy of Shutterstock.com

Joba Chamberlain's father Harlan has lived a life directly out of the Old Testament, a Job-like existence. A victim of polio when he was nine-months-old, Harlan was doomed to rely upon crutches and later a motorized scooter — that and also having Joba becoming his limbs for him at times. As a teen living in a children's home he was repeat-edly beaten and robbed by two bullies (until he got revenge by taking them on one at a time with his only good hand). His left hand became withered, and he was unable to grip a baseball with it. When he played catch with Joba, (somewhat like Pete Gray, a one-armed outfielder) Harlan caught the ball in his glove and tucked it under his chin; then after removing his glove, he would toss the baseball back to Joba. His left leg was also useless, so his son's throws had to be in the vicinity of Harlan's glove or Joba would have to fetch the ball before their games of catch could resume. He was deaf in one ear. His wife left him to raise Joba alone. And toss in poverty to the mix of woes—their tiny house had a bed which father and son had to share and their baseball equipment was castoff stuff bought at a yard sale for $3.

Joba's father never let his son forget their American Indian heritage (which included tales of American Indians such as ex-major leaguers Jim Thorpe, Allie Reynolds, and Chief Bender). He taught Joba sensitivity and responsibility, and in return Joba gave him unabashed admiration and love. As a child Joba and dad had a tender nightly ritual, exchanging "I love yous", "good nights", and "sweet dreams." Gary Smith wrote that Harlan lavished so much love on Joba that "he bounced right back even when the father growled too loud over a lapse of effort on the ball field."

Learning how his father had to live in five foster homes after polio claimed his parents, had to battle death, and had to endure more than a dozen operations as a child gave Joba deep insights into life. No self-pity for the Chamberlains—you'll never hear them wail, "If it wasn't for bad luck I wouldn't have no luck at all."

Joba, whose real name is Justin, was so hungry for baseball he continued to play catch with dad through even the harshest weather. Harlan, when not working as a unit manager at a state penitentiary, would make himself available for hours of catch. Often Joba would gather up baseball equipment while Harlan, who would act as the umpire and informal coach, would roll through the neighborhood like a motorized Pied Piper drumming up enough kids to play.

So committed to dad was Joba, he even stuck with him during the period when his friends were hanging out at the mall or out on dates.

As Smith's *Sports Illustrated* article put it, peer pressure could not "peel the son apart from his pop." Despite Joba failing to make his school's J.V. team two years in a row or, at the age of fourteen, lugging around so much *avoirdupois* that he nearly required oxygen when he scored a run, he was nevertheless destined for greatness.

After graduation Joba worked for the Lincoln Parks and Recreation Department, earning money to help dad pay their bills. All the while Harlan encouraged him: "You're one of the best, son. . . . You have the talent and the love—you've just got to believe it." Meanwhile Joba's would respond , "Dad, be real! You're going to say that, you're my dad."

At Nebraska-Kearney, a Division II college, Joba's fastball topped out at a modest eighty-four mph and he was bombed in his first outing (eleven runs in 1 1/3 innings). Still, dad exhorted, "If you endure the trials and tribulations and learn from them, nothing is insurmountable. Nothing."

Joba shed forty pounds and grew to six foot two and in 2005, after transferring to Nebraska, he was blistering radar guns at ninety-eight mph and helping the Cornhuskers to the College World Series with his 10-2 record. A $1.1 million pro signing bonus followed even after Joba underwent knee surgery and Harlan had to serve as Joba's legs in a role reversal. Harlan would wake up every few hours night after night to help ice his son's knee.

In 2006 an incident occurred which left Joba terrified that he was about to lose his father. Joba received a phone call from dad pleading for him to hurry home. Joba found his father there in agonizing pain. He rushed him to the hospital where Harlan's appendix soon burst. Complications ensued and death was a near-reality. Harlan spent nine days on a ventilator and five months in the hospital.

When Joba became a father that year, he said of his father, "I'll settle for being half the dad he's been." The following year at the age of twenty-one, Joba jumped three rungs in the Yankees minor league ladder, recorded an 18-to-1 strikeouts-to-walks ratio in Triple A ball with control as sharp as a buccaneer's cutlass, and then made the ultimate step by getting called up to the parent club. There, sometimes reaching the 100 mph plateau and mixing in a wicked slider, he fanned twenty men in his first fifteen 1/3 innings pitched—all shutout innings at that. Batters were overpowered by his fastballs and immobilized by his straightjacket-like sliders.

Late in that season Joba, with a doctor's approval, took dad to see a Yankees game in Kansas City. During batting practice players trotted by to greet Harlan and praise him for the tremendous job he did rearing Joba. That night, with the Yankees nursing a 3-2 lead, Joba was called in to pitch. Dad looked on, tears cascading down his cheeks. Joba worked two shutout innings and New York held on to win.

After the Yankees wrapped up their 2009 World Championship on November 4th in a six-game series against the Philadelphia Phillies, Joba was on the stage which had been set up for the post game festivities. Amid a mob of the media he was waving a Yankee flag to celebrate the moment. After spying his father, Joba leapt from the stage, rushed to Harlan and embraced his best friend with an ursine-like hug. Then, to describe the scene paraphrasing the shortest verse in the Bible, they wept. "We did it, dad," Joba shouted. Harlan, like a choir member repeating a refrain, responded, "We did it."

Harlan would later relate how he had told Joba over the years that he would some day win it all: "We talked about getting to the World Series all the time. We just shared that moment while realizing that he did it. I pinched myself a few times. It's pretty awesome. We love each other very much. The whole adventure in life is about family, and in our case, it's about father and son." Regrettably, Joba's mother was absent because she was in trouble with the law.

In June of 2011, when the Chamberlains learned that Joba had sustained a torn ligament in his right elbow that would require Tommy John surgery and place him on the sidelines for the duration of that season, Joba faced it with typical stoicism and determination. Harlan noted, "Now that he's facing what every pitcher doesn't want to face, he's going to face it with a positive attitude. Let's get it done." That sentiment typified the Chamberlain never-quit attitude as father and son embarked on the healing process, a process they had faced many times before and in many ways.

Adrian Gonzalez

The Adrian Gonzalez saga begins in San Diego (where he was born), has stops in Tijuana, Mexico, then back to San Diego, where he wound up playing for the Padres, and ends most recently in Boston. (However, if he keeps up his fabulous play, his baseball terminus will be Cooperstown, New York.)

Adrian couldn't have chosen a better father or family for that matter. Adrian says of his father David, "I grew up with a great father and I'm real thankful for him—just a great role model." His father sells air conditioners, and along with Adrian's two older brothers, also runs the Gonzalez Sports Academy. Quite simply, baseball is in his family's blood. His oldest brother, David, Jr., and Edgar, the middle of the three Gonzalez sons, have played pro baseball. Edgar, in fact, was once Adrian's teammate on the San Diego Padres and still plays the game. He began the 2011 season in the San Francisco farm system, playing at the Triple-A level for the Fresno Grizzlies at the age of thirty-three, four years older than Adrian.

Adrian, a modest man from humble roots, said his childhood was typical in that he played baseball games with his father. Adrian explained, "For the most part we wouldn't really sit down and watch games at home. It would be more like him taking us to games or we would be playing. He managed the team I played for one year and he was always around watching or playing his own games."

Adrian actually grew up on both sides of the San Diego-Tijuana border and had his first baseball experience at the age of five in San Ysidro. When he turned ten he played baseball in the summer in San Diego and in Tijuana during the year's other seasons. On some overlapping occasions he'd play games in both venues on the same day, switching his uniform in his father's car as they crossed the border.

Adrian was around twelve years old when he played on a team managed by his father, a man who certainly knows the game of baseball. Having played amateur ball as a member of the Mexican National team, he had a solid background and he truly loved the game, a game which the Gonzalez family all agree helped them to bond.

Edgar noted baseball is all the three sons have known: "All our conversations were usually baseball when we were young. It was all about baseball—that was our whole life."

Adrian added, "By the time I came around, everybody was always engulfed in baseball. So there was nothing you could do but continue the tradition and just love the sport. . . .". As if to overemphasize his point, he added, "It was always just baseball, baseball, baseball."

Adrian said one of his earliest and certainly one of the best recollections he had of his father and of how baseball tied the two together was when "all three of us [the three brothers] and my dad were on the same team—I think that was the best thing." That, too, took place in the amateur league in Mexico. Adrian remembered, "I was fifteen, Edgar was nineteen, David [Jr.] was twenty-three, and my dad was forty-something. He played D.H. at that time, but he was a first baseman growing up. It was four [of us] guys in a nine man lineup so we pretty much batted close to each other."

Adrian's father recalled that the game was a terrific experience and it fulfilled one of his goals in life: "to see them play on the same team with me." Priceless.

Baseball truly was a family act for the Gonzalez family, an act which dates all the way back to the good old early games of Wiffle ball played with his brothers. Later, not very long after the Gonzalez family moved back North from Tijuana to the San Diego area, David erected a batting cage for his sons' use. Over the years the boys ripped so many wicked line drives in the cage that the nets became frayed and balls began to whistle through the holes in the netting. It got to the point where the cage was only used for batting practice for Wiffle ball contests.

Edgar said that when he defeated Adrian in those contests the younger brother would invariably begin crying, hating to lose even as a youngster. Even armed with the information that he would be expected to lose, since he was four years younger than Edgar, Adrian did not use excuses nor accept defeat. As a matter of fact, Edgar said Adrian would go off on his own to work on his game in order "to try to get something, an edge, to try to go ahead and beat me."

Edgar also said that while Adrian's fires burn blowtorch hot, they remain under the surface. Even when the two of them were out running Adrian might say that he's not really competing with his brother, but, Edgar explained, "when somebody goes ahead of him, he's pushing himself even more."

As a boy in Tijuana Adrian played baseball until dark—no, beyond when darkness set in. When he and his brothers were finally forced indoors they played impromptu games of baseball using anything: from a pair of socks rolled up into a ball-like projectile, to old tennis balls, and a toy bat or a makeshift one—a pillow. Typical of so many little boys, the Gonzalez kids would pretend to be their favorite baseball stars when they took their cuts, assuming the stance and style of, say, Tony Gwynn or Ruben Sierra.

Once when Adrian made an error in T-ball, he went home and threw a tennis ball off the wall in his home over and over and over again. Such was his extremely early commitment to the game and to himself. Edgar called him very competitive, and then threw in, "Stubborn. Hardworking always. Responsible."

Such zeal and preparation for the opposition, says Edgar, is still a part of Adrian, whether he is working out or watching footage of the pitchers he is about to face—he is always looking for any advantage he could gain.

Adrian said he certainly doesn't weep any longer or "throw fits or pout," having put that aside when he grew up. Adrian explains his intense reactions were a part of his youth, "That's why he [Edgar] rubbed it in and made sure it hurt me when I lost."

Adrian, a rather reserved adult, called himself an "even-keeled" person in that he doesn't tend to get very demonstrative about a victory in a given game or about making a single great play, or even those occasions when he doesn't come through. No slamming of his helmet or cries of anguish follow a bad at bat, but again, deep inside his emotions flow. "I'm going to be frustrated, but I'm not going to show it," he stated. He remains true to himself no matter what.

As far back as his high school days, Adrian refused to become someone he wasn't. His football coach expected him to be a holler guy, to chew out teammates who faltered, and to exhort those who needed a boost. Adrian simply turned to his coach and said, "That's not me," and he walked away from the game of football. Adrian considered himself to be "a soft-spoken leader," not a rah-rah type of guy.

Football days over, Adrian dedicated himself entirely to baseball—not a bad choice. At Chula Vista, California's Eastlake High, he hit a torrid .645 as a senior and was tabbed *The San Diego Union-Tribune* Player of the Year.

Even though Adrian became a first baseman like his father, he said it wasn't as if his father gave him copious tips about the position but he sure did "hit me a ton of ground balls." It paid off, although Gonzalez added that his smooth glove is a result of God-given ability (via good genetics) along with hard work: "My two older brothers are middle infielders—we're all infielders so it was a lot of ground balls and a lot of throws growing up."

David did give some hitting tips; the most basic one, which has lingered with Adrian to this day, was "just get a good pitch to hit."

Adrian also believes his father impacted him in other ways that go beyond baseball fields: "I think more than anything else it was his example of how he's generous and always doing whatever it takes to help. That's the biggest thing I've learned from him. Anybody's actions speak louder than words—anybody can say anything they want, you've got to show by doing it."

Sure, David wanted his sons to be good ballplayers, but there was much more than that. Adrian explained, "His biggest thing was he wanted people to say that we're good people rather than good players."

Adrian speculated that if someone asked his father about the one thing he was most proud of concerning Adrian it would be a quality such as compassion. Adrian believes his giving and caring nature came from his father. One salient example of that attitude is the foundation Adrian and his wife Betsy started, an organization which helps underprivileged youngsters through sports, health, and education.

David was once asked about his pride in Adrian and said that he doesn't pay much attention to the fact that his youngest son picked

Photo Courtesy of Brian Babineau/ Boston Red Sox

baseball as his means of making a living and that he has, in fact, become enormously successful in that field. Instead his pride stems, for each of his sons, from them being outstanding people.

"I'm happy that Adrian is doing what he's doing," David began, "but I'm not saying, 'Hey, hey, my son is a baseball player.'" He continued: "I think he is doing what he is capable of doing, and I'm proud of him being the guy he has to be."

Many fathers would find it difficult to stay grounded if their son was as talented and wealthy as Adrian. After all, Adrian entered 2011 having signed a seven-year contract (running through 2018) with Boston for $154 million, an astronomical sum for a man not born to wealth. Actually, it's an astronomical chunk of cash for just about anyone without a surname such as Buffett or Gates.

The Red Sox craved Gonzalez. Craved? It was more like they salivated sloppily over the prospect of adding and keeping his stick in their already-potent lineup. After all, they figured Gonzalez was already one of the game's most dangerous batters while playing his home games in hitter-hostile Petco Park in San Diego. What havoc could his bat unleash in cozy Fenway Park? Moreover, he was a Gold Glove caliber fielder. He soon proved himself capable of performing any act on a baseball field short of levitation.

Just three years removed from a season in which he drove home 119 runs for the Padres—nineteen percent of all his team's runs to top the majors—he didn't disappoint. He hit forty points higher than his .298 average in 2010 to finish at .338, second in the league. He threw in 117 RBI, just two off the league lead, and a major league high 213 hits.

Again, personal accomplishments can be discarded. Gonzalez places higher value on family. Adrian said that his dad was the kind of man who "worked a lot" and raised a strong family. "When he needed to let us know that he needed to discipline us, he did. My mom was the one there most of the time, but we always respected him because we knew that if raised his voice it was because he was mad. He didn't do anything to us in the way of disciplining us in a certain way, but he was always there with us—just a great father.

"I was a good kid, I mean I had three great examples by my two older brothers and dad as far as older men and they've all shown me the way."

Reminiscing further, Adrian summed up some pleasant thoughts about his father, memories he will never forget: "He was always a great guy and not just the time when we were able to play together." He added that, big leaguer or not, he is unafraid to use the word "love" in connection with his dad: "Yeah. I think it's something that anybody who grew up with a great dad like I did loves their dad." He went on to say that without his parents "and their time and love, I wouldn't be where I am."

Separated by many miles during the baseball season, Adrian said he still sees his father when possible, "but in the offseason I see him quite a bit—we get together."

No wonder.

Josh
Hamilton

Photo Courtesy of Brad Newton/ Texas Rangers

B orn in Raleigh, North Carolina, to Linda and Tony Hamilton, Josh had good bloodlines. Linda, for example, played on her high school's *boys* varsity baseball team. Linda and Tony met at a ballpark; just after Tony finished warming up for his softball game, he noticed Linda crank two deep homers in her game on a nearby diamond.

As a six-year-old first grader, Josh practiced with his brother Jason's team, comprised of kids as much as six years older than Josh. The team was coached coached by their dad, a man who knew the game, despite not having played baseball in high school. When Josh played in Little League, on a team also coached by his father, his throws from shortstop sizzled so much he injured teammates. Tony, who grew up big and strong on a chicken and hog farm (he once bench pressed 540 pounds), insisted Josh be a leader and not let up on his throws or mighty swings. "You play the way you know how to play," he advised, "and avoid getting into bad habits." In his next practice he crushed the ball so hard his teammates backed up until nobody was manning the infield. Parents soon groused he was *too* good for the league and when an official concurred, Josh was moved up to play in Jason's league. His father, teaching his son a lesson about seniority, batted Josh ninth even when, a few weeks after his seventh birthday, Josh laced his first homer. Josh said he always wanted to please his father and recognized there'd be no favoritism played.

Around this time Josh began a habit of kissing his mother and maternal grandmother, Granny, who lived next door to him, prior to every game. From childhood on he has referred to his father as "Daddy." Josh was an All-American little boy, almost a Mamma's *and* Pappa's boy.

Josh later wrote of the many lessons he absorbed from his father as he grew up: to remain humble despite his status as a baseball wunderkind and to respect baseball and other people always, including opponents and umps. Both parents stressed that "a ballfield [sic] was the best place to be" and that playing sports keeps youths out of trouble. Tony, who ran highly disciplined teams, coached his sons on many a field until they reached high school.

Josh always understood the myriad sacrifices his parents made, scrimping to save money so they could afford to make trips to watch their sons play ball. Tony, a supervisor for a bread factory, often went in early—sometimes with only three hours of sleep—so he could wrap up a day's work before taking Josh to a game, which sometimes required a six-hour round trip. When Josh was twelve, a new boss told Tony he couldn't continue to work flexible hours. He challenged him, "What's more important, the ballgame or your job?" Tony unhesitatingly punched out, whirled out the door, and never returned. Family first.

That same summer Josh vowed to his parents, "If I get drafted and get some money, I want you guys to retire."

After playing football as a freshman, Josh, becoming "country strong" like his dad, decided to focus solely on baseball. Tony helped with strength training and on increasing bat speed. Confident his son had the right stuff, Tony had Josh prepare for the world of professional baseball, thinking of everything down to using wood bats, not aluminum ones.

At Athens Drive High School, Josh hit .636 and went 11-2 as a junior (his fastball would soon top out at ninety-seven mph): the first of two years he was his state's Player of the Year. When his pitching threatened to overshadow his hitting, his father, who knew Josh wanted to become an everyday big leaguer, told him to ease up just a bit, realizing the scouts would be tempted to make him pitch in the pros if he showed too much on the mound.

Baseball America's selection as the finest scholastic player in the country, Josh became the number one draft pick in 1999 just two days after graduation, earning him a $3.96 million dollar contract from Tampa Bay. Tony had helped instill confidence in Josh who, during his first press conference, unveiled his plans for his career. He estimated a three-year stint in the minors, a fifteen year big league tenure, and then, declared Josh, "I'll have to wait five years to get into the Hall of Fame."

The money he hauled down allowed his phenomenally supportive parents to leave their jobs and travel with Josh as he played minor league ball. Not only that, Josh would often stay in a hotel with his parents, not in the hotel where his teammates stayed. His parents were at each of his games, from batting practice through the final out; they and Josh were virtually inseparable. Tony even discouraged Josh from going out with teammates after games, realizing, prophetically it turns out, that post-game gatherings often have deleterious results on players' careers.

While critics felt his folks were suffocating him, Josh asserted they were never "stage parents"—the presence of his loved ones was both desired and appreciated. They were, he stated, supporting him, making "the transition easier," and never interfering. Josh also benefited from his dad's postmortems of his every at bat. In short, Josh felt that as a raw youth, "It felt good to look up into the stands and see two familiar faces."

When Hamilton won the Sally League's MVP trophy in 2000 his dad beamed, "You're on your way, Josh," and both felt big league success was inevitable.

In 2001 Josh and Linda were both injured when a truck rammed into their car, resulting in Linda's need for neck surgery and six months of recovery. They left Josh's spring training and returned home for Linda to get treatment for her neck. Injured and alone for basically the first time in his life (although Josh doesn't feel this was the sole reason for the start of his problem), he began drinking and taking drugs. He suggested other causes such as boredom, weakness, or perhaps even "something as superficial" as his penchant for acquiring a truckload of tattoos, beginning with six early in the 2000s (he wound up with twenty-six). Tony had said of the surprising new look of his son, "If this is the worst thing he ever does, I'll be happy." But many worse things did follow.

Josh started hanging out at a tattoo parlor with people who were every parent's nightmare, finding solace and escape in the needle while adding as many as four tattoos to his *Illustrated Man* look in a day. In 2001 he tried beer for the first time. He later wrote that on the same night he also tried, and loved, cocaine, changing into "a different person," and altering his life forever. The next several years were drug-ladened, injury-filled blurs and, even when not suspended for substance abuse, he played baseball only sparingly. He was, he later confessed, engaging in acts of "self-punishment, maybe even self-mutilation." He was, on several levels, hooked.

When the Devil Rays learned of Josh's problem they sent him to the Betty Ford Clinic, one of eight rehab facilities he would eventually enter. When he broke the news to his parents, who naturally blamed themselves, their fervent wish was to turn back time and prevent Josh's plight. Instead, worse times were directly ahead.

By 2004 not even the assistance of his parents, who Josh wrote had gone through a gamut of raw emotions and had tried different techniques to help him, worked. He dropped fifty-five pounds and squandered a heap of money due to his crack addiction (in 2005 he blew about $100,000 on drugs over a six-week binge). Failing yet another drug test he was slapped with his fifth suspension—this time for one year.

Eventually his new bride Katie booted him from their home. Eventhough he was sinking toward a personal nadir, as Tony put it, "I never gave up on him." Nevertheless, dad issued an ultimatum: "The last time I took him to rehab, I told him point-blank, 'Josh, this is it! If you don't want to change your life, I'm not going to change it for you.'" Not quite ready for the well-intended, tough-love routine, Josh continued to plummet into an abyss. At one point in 2005, not long before his daughter Sierra was born, he sank so low he traded Katie's wedding ring for drugs.

Finally, in despair, he moved in with Granny and later stated, "I was doing everything I could to kill myself," including using drugs under her roof despite her devotion to him and his recovery. Luckily, he came to realize how much he was hurting his loved ones and how he simply had to turn to God for help. In October of 2005 he went cold turkey.

His revival quickly began. He moved in with his wife and trained rigorously. By 2007 the man who, by his own reckoning, should have already been dead or in jail, was in the majors with the Reds. His resurrection seemed complete when, on Opening Day, he was engulfed by multiple standing ovations. During pre-game festivities when his name was first announced he glanced into the stands and saw his family, including his robust father, weeping openly.

The following season, after being swapped to Texas, he led his league in RBI (he had a staggering ninety-five at the All-Star break) after putting on a one-man pyrotechnic show during the 2008 All-Star Home Run Derby. His bat was as terrifying and as lethal as a firing squad, and with it he pounded out a single-round record twenty-eight homers, thirteen of them consecutive, with many peppering the upper deck. Each homer seemed as dramatic and as flamboyant as the final cymbal clash of our national anthem. Dad looked on, aglow with pride at Josh's slugging that day.

Josh, having been trained by his father to be respectful, had chosen his old American Legion coach, Clay Council, to throw to him in the derby—despite Clay's age of seventy-one. It proved to work out quite well for both Josh and his former mentor.

In another gesture of thanks Hamilton began sharing the message of his precipitous and perilous decline and of salvation, speaking to groups all over the country.

In 2011 Tom Grieve, who has spent nearly forty-five years in professional baseball with the Washington/Texas franchise, handling just about every job save dragging the infield, said that Hamilton "is someone that you have to admire for the way he's overcome adversity in his life. He still battles that addiction everyday, but he's regained his form and become one of the best players in baseball. He carried our team to the postseason [in 2010 when he won the AL MVP]." Grieve's words are a strong testimonial to both Josh *and*, indirectly but importantly, to Josh's father as well.

As Texas advanced through postseason play in 2010, Josh's teammates respected him so much they celebrated each round's victory twice—once with him present, using ginger ale as their spray of choice, and once after Josh departed the clubhouse, when they then broke out the champagne.

Now a solid family man, with a wife and three daughters, Josh perceives his life as a "cautionary tale." He still feels his future looks bright, despite a relapse he suffered in January of 2012 when he succumbed to temptation and went out drinking one night. His love for family remains strong, as he appeared genuinely contrite at a press conference in which he apologized for slipping. He seems destined to pass on the life lessons his father taught him—and the crueler lessons learned from his own mistakes—to his children.

Shelley
Duncan

D ave Duncan, who was first called up to the majors when he was only eighteen, caught for the Athletics, Indians, and Orioles. His final season was the year of America's Bicentennial. In 1979, his son Shelley was born and his son Chris followed a year-and-a-half later. Since then, Dave has done two things involving baseball and family which he greatly enjoys. He has served as the highly regarded pitching coach for close friend Tony La Russa on several clubs, and he has watched his sons grow into manhood, making their way into the major leagues.

Dave, along with just a few other men such as Leo Mazzone, is a rarity in that the average fan cannot name more than one or two pitching coaches. That position is, for the most part, an anonymous one. Dave, however, has excelled in that role for so long, producing (or certainly helping to develop) tons of standout pitchers, that his name is widely known and associated with excellence.

Often in the father-son relationship when the topic of pride comes up, it's the dad speaking of how proud he is of his offspring. Shelley, though, is the type of son who appreciates his father and the pride that flows in the family is a two-way street: "I am [very proud], but the stuff that I'm proud of is what I get to see behind the scenes. Our conversations, what he teaches me, the stuff I learn about him, how he was when he was a player.

"He's a very humble guy so it's hard for him to talk to me about himself. I learn from other people who have been around him. And whenever I get a chance to be around someone that spent a lot of time with him when he was younger, I always try to get as many stories as I can because they're always good."

Shelley and Chris, far from being boys now, both stand at six foot five and have, through 2011, a combined ten years of major league play behind them. Shelley plays somewhat sparingly, but productively. Dave defended him, saying he thinks Shelley's physique (230 pounds) has hurt his chances to play outfield full time. "You may be getting the job done," he observed, "but to the eye, it doesn't look pretty."

Shelley said he enjoys playing the outfield "because it reminds me of when I was a kid and I'd shag balls with my brother during Oakland A's batting practice," when his father coached there.

Shelley addressed an occupational hazard which goes with being in the big leagues—that of the father being away from family: "He was always gone during my brother and my baseball season. He missed out on a lot of stuff, but during the summers he'd always take us to the field and catch up with us and [play ball when possible]. He always kept us active in the game whether it's talking to us everyday when he was on the road about it or including us in what he does at work. He was always extremely active with us."

He was active, too, in helping guide his sons into becoming good people. Perhaps the most important lessons he tried to get across, said Shelley, were "basically, your actions everyday define who you are as a person, define your character. Go about your business the best you can every single day. Play hard every day when you're out there. Do whatever you can to make yourself available [for your team's manager]. There are times when I still screw up little things and he reminds me. A lot of good lessons."

In a world full of loud, brash athletes, Shelley, who took after his father, is a veritable relic, a modest, intense man who speaks softly, but definitely has something to say. As a kid, Shelley never went around acting like a big shot because his father had attained big league status. Dave told his son to stay humble, if for no other reason than because he had seen how often something comes along to knock a person down a peg or two. Shelley recalled his father telling him things such as, "Respect everybody, respect your coaches, respect your elders—listen to everybody. The more you listen to people, the more knowledge you'll get to create your own thoughts and feelings at a certain age." In short, Dave truly made it a point to lead his children into manhood.

Shelley noted that now that he is an adult he sees the groundwork his father established for him in a slightly different light than he did when he was a kid: "I think I can appreciate it in the sense of it set my foundation for a lot of stuff I do right now, and without it I might be a different person."

Dave was a pretty firm father, but Shelley describes his overall family situation thusly: "We had a very liberal household for as much trouble as my brother and I got into, but he [dad] was strict when he was around. We probably got into more trouble than we should have. I cost my dad a lot of money—me and my brother when we were younger. But the good thing was that it encouraged us to go out there and be kids. We were always outside, we were always playing, we were always doing something active. If it wasn't playing baseball, we were playing football or basketball or riding our bikes."

The boys possessed boundless energy. Always on the go, they were not unlike a squirrel scampering over hot embers, their sporting endeavors honing their natural abilities.

Duncan continued, "He encouraged us to always be doing something to make ourselves better at whatever we wanted to do. And it wasn't just baseball that he put the pressure on us, he wanted us to be good at anything we wanted to be good at, which was nice."

Even as a young boy, Shelley—born two days shy of exactly three years after his father played in his final major league game—was being exposed to inside information available to very few people. Shelley said, "Every night we would talk about the little nuances in the game that other people wouldn't see and he would also have us sit in on the meetings with the manager and general manager where they talk about good baseball stuff."

Thanks to such a background Shelley was capable of understanding baseball at a high level way before the other kids he played against. Furthermore, his baseball inculcation, albeit on a simplistic level back then, actually began when he was around three or four years of age. That's when he first visited major league clubhouses, starting with his father's days with the Chicago White Sox from 1983 through 1986 under La Russa, a manager who knows a good thing when he spots one. He has never been without Dave on his coaching staff, hiring him in Oakland (from 1986-1995) after his days in Chicago and moving over to St. Louis with Dave from 1996 through, to date, 2011.

"I remember those days, coming in every once in awhile," began Shelley. "I remember the [White Sox] clubhouse and the guys. Jim Leyland was the third base coach, Charlie Lau was the hitting coach." Not only could he learn from those men, but he was also exposed to Harold Baines, Carlton Fisk, Tom Seaver, and LaMarr Hoyt. Shelley said, "They had a great team and I have vague memories about that, but that was my intro into the baseball world."

Unlike many children, Shelley did not receive his first bat, ball, and glove from his father: "My grandpa [Shelley Richey] was mostly that one. My whole name is David Shelley—first name after my dad and my middle name after my grandpa. When my dad was away he was my man of wisdom that I'd go to for a lot of stuff. He lived a pretty good life himself. He didn't know baseball, but he knew how to be a man, that was for sure. He spent some years as a cattle rancher, a tank commander in the Army, he got a Silver Star and a bronze medal, and he spent some years being a lawyer in southern Arizona. He developed a really good reputation there himself, but I look at him as like he's, you know the commercial, the most interesting man? He had done all kinds of things. My grandpa had a very wide background; he taught me a lot about how to be a man and a lot of that stuff."

Specifically he instructed his grandson to speak his piece, not to hold things inside, and to be himself. Shelley noted how fortunate he was to have "two good people to have in my life as role models."

Dave always wanted Shelley to follow his path and become a catcher (which Shelley did in high school in addition to pitching), but that wasn't to be. At the University of Arizona he was an outfielder and a closer who topped out at ninety-four mph and who sometimes trotted in from the outfield to work late relief. "Then," said Shelley, "I blew out my elbow in my sophomore year and ended up playing right field."

Shelley continues to stay close to his dad and says they keep in phone contact every single day: "The older I get the more I'm proud of, not only what he does in the game of baseball right now, but who is he as a man. I want to live up to the reputation that he's worked so hard for, for himself. We share the same name, the same blood. And when he played, he played the game hard. He works as hard or harder than anybody and he's taught me to play the game the right way. So not only do I feel like I'm representing myself, I feel like I'm also representing the legacy that he's started."

Meanwhile, Chris, fittingly as the son of a pitching coach, began his baseball days on the mound. When asked how he wound up as an out-fielder he quipped succinctly, "I wasn't a very good pitcher."

Shelley's brother came a long way since the Cards picked him as a kid right out of high school in 1999 as a supplemental first-round pick. His big league debut came as a late season call-up in September of 2005 by the St. Louis Cardinals, the team his father was with. Chris enjoyed his first big moment with the Cards on the final day of the season when he hit his first big league homer, doing so in front of a delighted dad.

In 2006 Chris faced Randy Johnson in a spring training contest ver-sus the Yankees and seemed overmatched, thrust into a lefty-versus-lefty match-up against a pitcher ranked as one of the greatest ever. Chris put a positive spin on the situation: "It was a kind of win-win situation. He's a Hall of Famer. He's struck out so many people. If he strikes me out, I'm just one of thousands who have struck out against him." Sure enough, he did fan against the "Big Unit" in his first trip to the plate. Chris, using the type of thinking his father was proud of, adjusted to Johnson the next time up and lashed into a 2-0 fastball for a home run.

Across the field, perched on the top step of the dugout was Shelley who had made the trip with the Yanks (although he would not make the big club that year) to be there for the game which served as a sort of family reunion.

Chris caught a glimpse of his brother and noted, "He was just smil-ing a bit." When Chris finished circling the bases, a high five and a smile were forthcoming from Dave. Dave not only felt proud of Chris, he also felt gratified that he had been able to advise his son to "be ready to hit his fastball." Johnson said Dave had given Chris "a good scouting report."

In a May 2011 interview Shelley said that his father, who has been around the majors for an eon, had never seen him play in a big league game, not once, not even in a spring training contest. Then, choosing his words with care, he said that his father did see him play some base-ball, but not "until my freshman year in college. We started our season in January. He came to a game and I hit two home runs." Asked if it was simply a coincidence or if he was inspired by the occasion, Shelley smiled and commented, "[expletive], yeah, I was inspired. It was the first time my dad got to see me play."

On May 30, 2011, in Toronto, Shelley uncorked a mammoth home run, one that sailed majestically into the fifth level at the Blue Jays home park, Rogers Centre. That made him just the fifteenth player to launch a ball into that distant target. With typical modesty he said that hitting such a blast is fun, but just for the moment. After that it's elbowed out of the picture and he humbly moves on, focusing on his next at bat. Just as dad would have it.

Steve Garvey

When Steve Garvey wrote about his childhood experiences in *My Bat Boy Days*, his dedication to his children read in part, " . . . never stop dreaming and believe in God. . . . dreams really do come true. All my love." He also stated he felt his autobiography "is a great example of father and son relationship." He was correct.

He chronicled how his father (and his "number one hero") Joe, a bus driver in Tampa, often was assigned charter groups including several baseball clubs during spring training in Florida. By 1956 seven-year-old Steve, like his father, a Brooklyn Dodgers fan, had fallen in love with baseball.

That same year his father had helped organize a local Little League program. In March, Joe, seizing the opportunity for "a great father-son day," asked Steve if he wanted to skip school and accompany him as he transported the Dodgers from the airport to Al Lang Field in St. Petersburg for an exhibition game versus the Yankees. The only ground rule was for Steve to be respectful to the players and to say, "Yes, sir," and, "No, sir," to them.

The sight of such luminaries as Pee Wee Reese, Duke Snider, and Jackie Robinson emerging from the DC-7 with the Dodgers logo scrawled across the plane's body made Steve realize he was in the middle of a glorious page from baseball's history book. He later wrote that it was as if the players had "suddenly walked off the baseball cards I had in my pocket and come to life." And this was just the start.

As the players disembarked, they patted Steve on his head and Roy Campanella told Steve if he worked tirelessly at his game "maybe someday you'll be a Dodger." A polite throw-away line, perhaps, but it proved to be prophetic. In fact, Brooklyn's manager back then, Walter Alston, would become Steve's first skipper when he joined the Dodgers thirteen years later.

Steve was also assigned batboy duties that day in Tampa and warmed up Gil Hodges. He mingled with other players and observed the game intently; and, still weeks away from his first Little League game, he soaked up "more about the game than I ever could have on my own." It was an experience he would carry forever. A splendid gift from dad. He told his father it had been "the greatest day of my life."

Joe topped off the day by presenting Steve with bats (given to him by a clubhouse attendant) which had been used, and broken, in the game by Snider and Carl Furillo. When father and son returned home and shared their experiences with Steve's mother, it became, as Steve later wrote, "a special moment in our lives — just the beginning of a new direction for the Garvey family."

At bedtime Joe had to instruct Steve to wash his hands thoroughly, to rid himself of the redolent pine tar: "Son, you will probably never forget that smell for the rest of your life!"

Steve has always considered his father to be a warm person, a man of "quiet dignity" as well as his "mentor, confidant, and teacher (and occasionally a stern disciplinarian when necessary)."

Over the next six years the Dodgers requested the personable Joe to be their driver when they came to Tampa. He also drove for the Tigers, Reds, and Yankees on occasion and Steve always joined dad, with Joe condoning the act of playing hooky. Joe informed teams that Steve was a good batboy so he continued to handle those chores and meet even more players. All this, Garvey wrote, "Laid the foundation for a lifetime love affair with our national pastime," and for his general success in life.

Along the way, Steve may have missed some school, but he picked up his doctorate in baseball. Snider gave him a slew of hitting tips. Hodges gave him his first lessons on playing first base and those sessions, wrote Steve, put him "years ahead of the other kids." It was as if Joe had provided private tutors for Steve who would go on to win four Gold Glove Awards and led his league in hitting twice.

Steve's duties lasted five years until his playing Pony League ball took up so much time he could no longer commit himself to any more batboy days. His final game, between the Dodgers and Reds, found him feeling as if he was "actually a part of the team in a small way." He couldn't begin to imagine that he would become a huge part of the Dodgers in the next decade, but the groundwork had been laid. He had learned "from the best, not just how to play the game, but how to live life with grace and character."

Joe, as usual, looked on during his son's final day as batboy, beaming and reflecting how happy he was to have given his son such a fantastic opportunity. He flashed Steve "a smile that only a dad can give." Later Steve would thank his parents for providing him with "a life that made dreams come true." He also said that he was driven to make his dream of being a big leaguer come to fruition for his father's sake.

Once a pro, Steve, like Joe, constantly displayed his hard working ways, rarely taking a day off—he even established the National League record for playing in the most consecutive games (1,207). Having his bat in the lineup each day was as comforting to his teammates and manager as a mother's lullaby.

Long ago Jackie Robinson taught Garvey how to predict what pitch an opponent was likely to throw in any given situation, a talent Steve has since passed on to his son Ryan, a young man who has evolved into a talented power hitter.

Ryan's Palm Desert High School coach, Darol Salazar, said he is "probably faster and has a better arm than his father." Steve has no problem with that assessment. "I want Ryan to be better than I was—any father would. We talk about having a pro game . . . it means hitting behind a runner to move him up, and making your teammates better. . . . We talk about measuring his success by the success of the team, because everything is measured by winning."

Salazar, a lifelong Dodger fan, stated Ryan and Steve "are very close and I noticed that from the first time I saw them. Steve is a really down-to-earth guy. When Ryan gets into the batter's box his mannerisms are identical to how his father hit." He asked Steve if Ryan, one of the hardest working kids he ever coached, made an effort to duplicate his looks at the plate. Steve replied, "That's all genetics." Salazar went on to say, "I think he did a great job of teaching Ryan respect of the game and they have a lot of respect for each other—they care a lot about each other.

"I've had other kids who had successful parents and they were in their shadows—they struggled to live up to expectations the public has. I never got that impression from Ryan; he was his own guy. He stood on his own and his dad did nothing but encourage him. Steve used to come to our practices and he just would watch—he would never, ever overstep his bounds, which was great."

On June 3, 2011, Ryan, wearing the same number his father wore (#6), played in California's Section Division IV title game held at his dad's old home ballpark, Dodger Stadium. It was an historic occurrence that Steve said meant a lot to him and his deceased father even though the 10-time All-Star said that watching Ryan play isn't easy. "It's like giving birth," he observed.

In 2010 Ryan went into a slump as a junior, perhaps because he was caring for and fretting about his grandfather. Visiting Joe at his hospice, Ryan shaved him and tenderly held his hand, the epitome of a devoted grandson. When cancer claimed Joe, Ryan, unwilling to let go, climbed into bed with him.

Ryan, strong but lacking his dad's Popeye-esque forearms, has had the advantage of talking with superstars of the past and of watching video of his father hitting. He translated all that into winning stats: during his first twenty-nine games as a senior he was flirting with a .400 and had driven in nearly one and a half runs per game. The Phillies liked what they saw and drafted him in 2011.

Steve never boasted of his accomplishments to his son, leaving it to Ryan to discover just how good dad was. He had witnessed people asking his father for his autograph, but didn't understand dad's status until he was about eleven years old and began "looking up stuff that he did. Then I'd joke with him and say, 'Appreciate that, thanks for telling me.'" By the age of thirteen Ryan finally understood enough about baseball to say to Steve, "Dad, you were pretty good, weren't you?" Raised to be humble, Steve has passed that trait on to Ryan.

Steve and wife Candace also taught the importance of knowledge, diligence, and, as Steve said, "being the best player on the field. Don't try to be 'Steve Garvey's son' every time up, because I tell him he can only put expectations on himself: be Ryan Garvey."

Ryan admitted that he does experience some pressure; much of it put there himself. Steve tried to ease Ryan's burden, by explaining, "I'm Ryan's father first; I'm dad. And if he wanted to pursue baseball, that was fine. If he didn't, Candace and I were OK with that, too."

And so the father-to-son chain of love and lessons of life and baseball continues: Joe-to-Steve-to-Ryan.

Chris Perez

Photo Courtesy of Tim Perez

When Chris Perez enters a game from his berth in the Cleveland Indians bullpen, he does so with a ninety-five mph fastball that explodes with the quickness of a cobra. Toss in an intimidating look, complete with his wild hair which cascades to his shoulders and his shaggy black beard, and he creates quite an appearance on the hill.

No wonder an observation made by one of Perez's former catchers spawned his nickname, "Pure Rage Perez." The reliever said of that moniker, "It kind of adds to the mystique when I come out there." Some fans label him the real Rick Vaughn, the over-the-top character played by Charlie Sheen in the motion picture *Major League*. Perez embraces that comparison.

Perez is successful now, but when he first got the call from the Cleveland pen in 2009 he bombed. His initial outing alienated some fans who were searching for a bullpen savior. He worked just two-thirds of an inning and gave up four runs after hitting two batters, uncorking two wild pitches (perhaps the song *Wild Thing* should have been blaring over the public address system), giving up two hits, and forgetting a pitcher's fundamental duty: covering first base on the back end of what might have been a double play.

His next few mound appearances didn't go well either, but Perez, who says he comes from a "strong family," didn't flinch; nor did he hide from the scrutiny of the media. Bill Lubinger of *The Plain Dealer* wrote that Perez didn't pull any punches either. For example, at one point he suggested his "catcher should have blocked a pitch in the dirt that set up the winning run." Chris's father Tim stated, "Well that's from me [Chris's outspokenness]. I've always told him, 'If you believe in something, then stand behind it.'"

Although Tim—once a catcher for Manatee Junior College and now a general contractor—didn't fulfill his dream of making it to the "Show," he taught the game to his son, starting with his days of coaching Chris when he was four years old through his junior year in high school. Tim also supported his son unreservedly. Chris recalled, "He provided me the opportunity to go to IMG, [the IMG Pendleton School] and I am sure that is not cheap. He paid for everything, all my equipment and summer ball and never told me 'no'."

Tim was kept busy when Chris was growing up. In addition to helping him with baseball, he watched Chris played football, basketball, soccer, and volleyball before Chris shoved all other sporting interests aside for baseball by around the age of thirteen.

As a boy, Chris, like dad, was a catcher. In high school, Chris caught (when not pitching) and hit with power, once blasting a home run ball, high off a light standard. Being a catcher taught Chris, who attributes his work ethic to dad, how to think along with hitters, a skill which paid dividends when he became a professional pitcher.

Tim felt Chris was best suited to pitch. Chris disagreed. When you're a kid, you don't always see or appreciate the legacy your father is passing on to you. Tim said that despite the fact that Chris could fire a ninety-mph fastball when he was a high school freshman, his son was reluctant to be locked into the role of a pitcher: "He fought us for awhile because he wanted to hit."

By Chris's senior year, though, his days as a position player were through. Dad had got the message across. "He sat me down," said Chris, "and laid it all out and said 'If you pitch, you might be able to make it to the big leagues.'" Chris later admitted that the position switch was wise: "I don't know how far I could have gotten as a catcher. Obviously, not to this level."

From the Florida high school mounds of Manatee and the Pendleton School at IMG Pendleton School where he played as a senior, it was on to the University of Miami where he was first used as a starting pitcher, but Chris noticed he wasn't effective late in games, probably because he went all out all the time. "I don't like holding anything back. I don't like having to pace yourself as a starter. . . . I like facing them with my best stuff right away," he stated. When the Hurricanes's closer went down due to injury, Perez asked to be moved into his role.

Tim had serious qualms about his son working out of the bullpen because he felt big league scouts tend to look more for starting pitchers. However Chris remained adamant. As Tim recalled, "He said, 'Dad, my dream is to be the last guy on the mound striking the last guy out.'"

All their hours of work came to fruition when Chris, a father himself now (his son Maxwell was born in 2010), was drafted by the St. Louis Cardinals in the first round of the 2006 June Amateur Draft. He spent twenty-five games in "A" ball at Quad Cities, but soon, to his father's delight, ascended the ladder to Triple-A ball, spending part of 2007 and all of 2008 with Memphis.

During the 2009 season Chris had to learn how to pack a suitcase quickly—he spent the year with Memphis, the Cards, and the Indians. With Cleveland, the six foot four, 230 pound Perez did nothing very special, turning in one save over thirty-two appearances to go with an 0-1 record and an ERA of 4.32.

His outings with Cleveland were far from stellar, but he hung in there, eventually moving from being a setup man to being the team closer when Kerry Wood was traded to the New York Yankees in 2010. Perez then went on to rack up twenty-three saves and a stingy ERA of 1.71 which ranked second among all AL relievers. Over one stretch of twenty appearances he did not give up a single run. He had arrived.

Chris said that his motivation to battle against the best baseball players in the world is his love of competition and winning, but, "Actually, I hate to lose more."

When his unheralded Indians bolted out of the 2011 starting gate they rattled off thirty wins over their first forty-five

games to turn the standings in the American League Central Division upside down.

Perez, who had been signed to a $1.8 million raise in January of 2011, sizzled. On April 30, the Indians—in existence since 1901—established a new franchise record for their most wins during the opening month of a season, 18. By May 23, when Cleveland held the best record in baseball, Perez had already chalked up thirteen saves and had taken part in exactly half of his team's thirty victories.

Although Cleveland faltered late in the year, they forged their early record despite dire pre-season predictions calling for a last place finish. As Tim put it, "When he's comfortable and feels good about what he's doing, that's what you're seeing now." He would finish with thirty-six saves.

Perez became an All-Star for the first time in 2011, and, through the break, he had converted thirty-one of his previous thirty-two save opportunities. What's more, when clinging to a slim one-run lead, he had been able to slam the door on opponents in nineteen of his previous twenty such outings. On a sad note, he discovered he had made the All-Star team on his way back to rejoin the Indians after attending his grandmother's funeral in Florida.

Photo Courtesy of Tim Perez

After the mid-summer classic Chris presented his father with his All-Star ring, a gift which brought tears to Tim's eyes. Chris explained, "I couldn't do anything else but give him the ring. He taught me the game. If it wasn't for him and all the sacrifices he made for me, I would not be where I am today. The ring is a thank you for everything he did for me."

Tim said he wears the ring constantly, "I always wanted to play major league baseball, but couldn't make it. Chris made it for both of us. I am living that through him. I am proud of it and proud of my son."

One cause for his pride is that his son remains unaffected by his success. Tim commented, "Even at the All-Star Game, he is still the same person to me. He is my kid and has not changed. He gets paid well, but it's not like he shows it. He takes care of his family and has a nice home. He is a normal kid, who happens to have a gift."

As for Chris's son, it's much too early to predict what caliber athlete he will become. However, in a 2011 interview with *The Plain Dealer*, Chris stated that being a new father is quite the experience: "Everybody says it changes your life and they're right. But it's not in a bad way, it's in a great way. . . . Whatever happened on the field, good or bad that day, you get home and he just smiles at you. He doesn't care."

It probably won't be too many more years before Chris's son will tag along, hand-in-hand with his dad, perhaps the owner of an All-Star ring from dad. He will, not unlike a duckling which has gone through the imprinting process, toddle behind Dad into a big league clubhouse and into his own bright future.

Fortunately for Chris and Maxwell, they live in an era in which baseball's management is understanding about, or at least tolerant of the importance of family to big leaguers. That certainly has not always been the case. Mike Hargrove recalled the time when players had to fight for something as simple as taking a day off for the birth of a child. One of Hargrove's teammates in Cleveland, Alan Bannister, once asked his manager if he could have permission to go home to be there when his wife Vicky delivered their baby. The manager's sarcastic reply was, "What are you, a doctor?" And when Hargrove's father-in-law passed away in 1976 he was granted permission to attend the funeral, but said that permission was granted very reluctantly. The front office sensed, as Hargrove put it, that if the OK "wasn't given, I was going to go anyway."

In 2011 Major League Baseball actually instituted a new acceptable reason for a player to leave his club: paternity leave. Any player may take twenty-four to seventy-two hours away from his club for the birth of a child; no balking by the club permitted, no questions asked. In April of 2011 Colby Lewis of the Texas Rangers became the first big leaguer to take advantage of the new rule, figuratively blazing a trail, hacking that path through baseball's antiquated value system. Other devoted fathers soon followed the lead of pioneer Lewis. The official stance by Major League Baseball was that, "Baseball understands that players need to be with their families. . . ."

That is something Tim and Chris have long understood.

Luis Gonzalez

On June 26, 1998, something occurred which forever altered the life of Luis Gonzalez—and it had nothing to do with baseball. It was on that day that Gonzalez, like former pitchers Dave Righetti and Dennis Cook, became the father of triplets (in the case of Gonzalez, via in-vitro fertilization). Of course, Melvin Mora had them all beat—he is the father of quintuplets; and, as an aside he was once traded for Mike Bordick, who is the father of twins. Imagine the logistics involved when those families had to move after that deal! Luis and wife Christine named their children Megan, Alyssa, and Jacob (who, as a three-year-old took to calling his bedroom the dugout).

Even after enduring a bad day at the ballpark, Luis said coming home to his children erased all woes and pressures. "I used to stress out and sit up all night thinking about the game. I'd go nuts if I made an error or threw an at bat away," said Gonzalez in a 2001 interview. "Now I'm just Dad. How can you be mad after you see them? They put it all in perspective."

The babies' arrival also required Luis to purchase five cases of formula and 252 diapers every week. He quipped, "Changing diapers is like working on an assembly line. Once you get the third baby done, the first one is ready to be changed again." When bedtime rolled around the five peas cuddled together with their parents, though not always comfortably, in their pod: two queen mattresses pushed together. Christine commented, "You get a few knees and elbows to the face."

The affable Gonzalez sports an almost perpetual smile and was perhaps the most cooperative and generous player of his day, although among opposing pitchers on game day he was about as welcome as a card counter in Vegas. He felt a power boost he believed was at least partly attributable to fatherhood. He went from being an almost insignificant player (he was once traded for Karim Garcia) who typically hit about ten homers per season over the first half of his career, to becoming a bona fide power threat who posted twenty-three, twenty-six, and fifty-seven home run seasons after becoming a parent. He even ripped a record-tying thirteen homers in April of 2011. Such glamour (and subsequent wealth) didn't change much at home—he still treated his family to lunch almost daily, often dining at the kids' favorite spot, Chuck E. Cheese's.

His wealth did, however, allow him to become more generous. For instance, when Gonzalez first realized just how big a fan the D-backs clubhouse doorman was, he went out and purchased a TV for him to watch during their games. He frequently picked up hefty dinner tabs for teammates even when he wasn't eating in the restaurants and tipped clubhouse attendants as much as $100 for running simple errands. He commented, "I'm no different from anybody else. I treat Joe, the door guy, the same way I treat Randy Johnson or Curt Schilling. That's the way I was brought up." Additionally, he lent his name and time to many causes such as the Make-A-Wish Foundation and the Boys and Girls Clubs.

As for his own childhood, the man known as "Gonzo" felt that he was blessed to have been born in Tampa, an area teeming with baseball tradition. He said, "I had a unique opportunity, growing up in Florida, being around spring training my whole life. One of the funny things was being able to get out of school sometimes. You know, your parents would take you out to go out to see the spring training games and that was a big thrill for me; just being able to see players that you idolize. I grew up in Tampa where the '75 Big Red Machine [Cincinnati Reds] was [training]. Your parents are your role models and your heroes, but these are the guys who you would you love to go home and imitate and pretend like you're those guys—even after the games, late at night playing Wiffle ball or stickball or whatever you would do. So it was a fun learning experience going to games, especially with your parents."

He continued, "What was funny is I played with Tino Martinez in high school and we would be the guys that went to watch those games. Whether it was "A" ball, the Tampa Tarpons when they were there [or Reds' spring training] you just get excited. I still remember as a kid, I could rattle off just about the whole starting lineup for those guys. They were just a group of guys that got along well together and gelled well together and were able to bring a lot of championships to Cincinnati where there's a rich tradition of baseball."

Gonzalez later helped bring a title to Phoenix with the signature moment of his career: his Game Seven, ninth-inning base hit off Yankee closer Mariano Rivera to hand the Diamondbacks—in just their fourth year of existence—the world championship in 2001. Sheer drama. Gonzalez said that while his childhood fantasy was, naturally, belting a walk-off World Series homer, he gladly settled for his drama-packed bloop hit.

Back when Gonzalez was a boy and worked in a cigar factory run by Tino Martinez's grandfather, building up his muscles, he had a baseball idol: "Pete Rose was my guy and I've always enjoyed watching him play and now, as a thirty-four-year-old player in the big leagues in my thirteenth year [in 2002], that's kind of the mentality that you take. I mean, I don't have the same hustle style as him—you know, headfirst sliding and things like that, but that's the guy who, as a young kid, I would imitate his stance. . . . Obviously your styles change when you get older, but there are those guys who you looked up to and admired."

Like any big baseball fan, Luis was overjoyed when his parents, Ame and Emilio, both born in Cuba and both clearly very understanding people, "would take me out of school occasionally [to attend a game]. And you know what? I think where I grew up there were so many players that have played in the big leagues [roughly forty at the time of Gonzalez's comments] that the opportunity to go see a hometown guy or to see a big game [is why they let me go].

"And you know times have changed, there are so many more activities and different things going on out there, where I think a little bit of that father-son relationship has kind of lost its luster a little bit.

"But it's still fun even now as a player when you look into the stands and you see a dad with his kid or a grandparent. The father or the mom or the grandparent is teaching their kids the game. And even though you're on the other side of the coin, playing in the game, you're still human—I'm a parent, too, and you know what's going on out there [the bonding]."

Looking back once more, the bilingual Gonzalez reminisced, "My dad was a Little League manager or coach to me and there were a lot more demands at times because you're the coach's son and you're expected to go out there and play good, but it was fun.

"There were some tough times there where you just wanted to be just like any of the other kids. You have a lot of high expectations [of you] especially where I grew up, where to parents, baseball was not only young players' dreams, but it's almost like your parents kind of pushed you that way because they wanted you to try to be successful—trying to be the next guy to come out of that area. And like I said, where I grew up was a hotbed of baseball with your Dwight Goodens, your Dave Magadans, your Lou Piniellas, your Tony La Russas, Al Lopez, and guys like that. The list goes on and on. It's rich in tradition and it's a Hispanic area and [while] football is big in Florida, baseball to the Hispanic people is what everyone wanted to do. I've always followed it and I, even when I'm not playing, still enjoying rooting for guys that I admire as players."

In 2002 Luis spoke of his son's interest in baseball, "You know what, what's fun for me is when I get to bring him [Jacob] in here [the Arizona Diamondbacks clubhouse] after the game. He just turned four and he knows every one of the players' names. His favorite player is Craig Counsell and that doesn't bother me because he's a great role model to have as your favorite player. Obviously, I'm his father, but it's a comfortable warm feeling to know that your son admires other guys on the team and he likes doing the knuckles and the high-five [as a congratulatory greeting]." Of course, the year before Gonzalez made these comments, his triplets' favorite "player" had been team mascot D. Baxter the Bobcat.

"What's nice about this ball club that we have here," continued Gonzalez, "is it's older players, and a lot of guys have kids. . . . as players you learn to accept all the other kids running around here and you want them to remember you as a player and as a good person when they get older. You want their memories to be, 'Hey, I hung around Luis Gonzalez or Randy Johnson, or a Jay Bell or a Matt Williams, Steve Finley— guys like that.'

"Hopefully, one day when you're done playing, and if their kids eventually make it to the big leagues and you come in the locker room, you get to tease them a little bit, saying, 'I remember when you were the little runt running around the locker room.' Or, 'I remember that kid when he was running around here harassing and looking for stuff in my locker.' There are some players whose genes run deep and some of these kids will eventually make it to the big leagues." Gonzalez nailed it—baseball truly is a family affair.

CC Sabathia

CC Sabathia—(his real name is Carsten Charles Sabathia II)—is the son of a man who went by the nickname Corky—a man who, regrettably, didn't live to see the most glorious of CC's accomplishments. In fact, from the time CC was thirteen, when Corky and his wife Margie split up, until he was about twenty, CC saw his father infrequently—rarely could he gaze into the stands to see his father.

Margie, though, insisted they keep in touch by phone, and that, said CC, "kept our relationship going."

Then, in 1998 after CC graduated from high school, Corky, like a prodigal father, returned to CC's life. Not long after that he told his son he had HIV (he had waged a long-time battle with drugs) and said, "I'm going to need you to take care of me now and be the strong one." CC, numbed by the revelation, accepted the role reversal and later observed, "[I] was just glad I had a chance to be with him those last few years."

Margie was pleased about the reunion saying, "Every son needs a father," and she took pleasure seeing CC and dad together in spring training camp.

In 2003, on the very day CC learned Corky had terminal stomach cancer, he was also notified that he had made the American League All-Star squad for the first time. On a team flight—his baseball honors now meaningless, and with time for thoughts about mortality to settle in—he openly wept as he discussed his father's plight with a teammate.

CC and his wife Amber, who had been his high school sweetheart, were expecting their first child in about three months and CC's most fervent prayers were for a healthy baby and that Corky "would be able to see my son."

CC, whose father had moved in with him by this point, relished his dwindling but precious time with dad. CC told writer Buster Olney, "It felt like I was a kid again, having him around. We had long talks. We laid everything on the line, because he didn't know how much longer he'd be around. He was fighting to stay alive. I think he was holding on to see my son."

He made it—barely. When Carsten III was born, CC carried the infant to a contented Corky. Over the final weeks of Corky's life, CC further pleased his dad when he spoke of how it had been so important for the two of them to "get right with each other," to cement a wonderful relationship.

Being together up to the end also afforded Corky the chance to impart a final bit of advice. "Take care of your mom and your family, and make sure you do things the right way," said Corky, not long before he passed away in late 2003 at the age of forty-seven. CC now sports a tattoo under his right forearm to pay homage to his father.

Four years later when CC was selected to play in the 2007 All-Star Game in San Francisco, California, it instantly brought back a bittersweet memory involving his father. "The minute they built AT&T Park, my dad told me, 'Wouldn't it be great if they have the All-Star Game here and you pitch in it?'" related CC. Turning sentimental, he added, "I know he's somewhere watching." Clearly he was addressing a common father-son motif.

On a simplistic level, Corky, or, more accurately, photos of Corky, glanced down on his son each day from a cabinet door on CC's locker. "Look at him," said CC to Associated Press writer Tom Withers. He pointed to his favorite picture of Corky, a photo of him in an Indians uniform with CC's jersey number 52 on his back, of course. CC continued, "He was such a fan. He just loved it."

Corky truly had been prophetic about the 2007 mid-summer classic when he declared, "I know you're going to be there." He was also inspirational. Back then CC confessed, "That's all that I've been thinking about all year. Those words from him." Having grown up in nearby Vallejo, California, in the shadows of the Golden Gate Bridge, CC bought twenty-five tickets for the contests for family and for friends he wanted to take care of, wishing, of course, that his dad could also be on hand.

Had Corky been one-hundred percent prescient, he might have foreseen that CC would win 2007 Cy Young Award. CC, his left arm a rapid-fire Gatling gun, copped that honor several months later with his finest season to date (19-7).

Things weren't always so positive for him, though. As a 1998 first-round draft pick, he showed superb promise during his 2001 rookie season when he was twenty years old. However, after going 17-5, his stats slipped and his weight ballooned to 300+ pounds (as a junior in high school he stood six foot six and already weighed 245 pounds).

Baseball Dads

Photo Courtesy of AP Images

Then, after losing his father, uncle, and a dear friend over a short period of time, he sank to a mediocre 11-10 season in 2004. He began getting rattled on the mound, frequently losing his temper—a problem which dates back to when he was around five years old—and his control. "I put way too much pressure on myself," he recalled. He even tipped his pitches and, according to his peers, was little more than a thrower, not a complete pitcher. By 2007, Mike Sweeney of the Royals, among others, saw a transformation. "Now," he observed, "he's working the corners." That prompted Withers to write, "Just like dad taught him to."

In 2007 CC Sabathia—now a parent capable of teaching his offspring a thing or two—proudly said, "I'm a dad and my son loves baseball and we enjoy going out in the backyard and playing." While his son CC Sabathia III, nicknamed "Little C," was only three years old at the time, CC said the boy already looked like an athlete: "I don't want to force it on him, but he's already pretty good. I'm sure he's going to play."

It harkened back to the days when CC was on youth league diamonds (and later on, high school football fields as an all-conference tight end who signed a letter of intent to play for the University of Hawaii). When he was eight he was already showing signs of athletic dominance.

There's no telling how big CC's children will become, but his mother Margie—whose father was almost exactly three inches shy of being a seven-footer—took to carrying around a copy of her son's birth certificate to prove he was indeed playing in the correct league and not cheating.

In 2007, CC also said that if his son should eventually possess the talent required, to play at the big league level, he would give him advice such as: respect the game and " be humble and play the game the right way.

"For me, my dad was really tough on me as far as coaching and things like that. I don't want to coach him [my son], I want to be Dad. I don't want to be on him everyday and tell him what to do because that kinda' gets old, but I want to be able to have a conversation about what happened during the game." And CC, when not playing a game himself, attends every sporting event his children engage in.

By the end of the summer of 2010, he and Amber had added three more children—Jaden, then five, Cyia, two, and a newborn, Carter—but he still held to his solid views on child rearing and the coaching of one's offspring.

Just as his parents had taught CC the importance of accepting responsibility and respecting others, so too will CC and Amber instill those and other values in their children.

CC, blessed with a strong foundation, was also fortunate that thanks to baseball, he has been able to raise his family in a $15 million home in a community which also was home to Britney Spears and Jay-Z—a startling contrast to the tough area he grew up in, which was no stranger to "drugs and violence on the streets."

Remembering his background, CC has given back to his community, buying baseball equipment for his old high school and paying for improvements to a youth league field in Vallejo, generous gestures which would have made his father proud; and the Sabathia legacy rolls on.

Michael Brantley

S oft-spoken but articulate, Michael Brantley is so appreciative of his dad, he comes across as *the* ideal son. Not all major leaguers in their early twenties are mature enough to realize and unashamedly express their appreciation for all their fathers have done for them. In an age in which too many athletes are brimming with a sense of entitlement, Michael and his attitude are refreshing.

When his father Mickey (officially he's Michael Brantley, Sr.) speaks, Michael listens. Part of the reason he is so attentive is because Mickey, a former big leaguer, has been through everything Michael is now going through—he's seen it all. Michael is following in his father's cleat prints, so to speak: "There's a handful of stories [my father told me]. We talk baseball almost every day. We always have good stories to tell, back and forth to one another and it keeps the conversation going. He's a great influence in my life."

Their conversations, including anecdotes and baseball situations, have taken place throughout Michael's life. Michael explains, "One of the greatest quotes I live by is one that he told me. He said, 'Whatever you do in life just make sure you give it 110 percent. I don't care if it's vacuuming the floor, to cleaning your own room, to playing baseball, to running down the line hard. Whatever it is, just give it 110 percent and at the end of the day, that night, you'll know you gave it all you got today.'

"He's a very levelheaded person. That's where I get my characteristics and my traits from. Everybody says I look so even-keeled and that's probably the reason: how I was brought up in the game. And I take my hat off to my mom and my father for that."

The pivotal father-son conversations often relate to things Mickey went through as a professional baseball player. Michael listens raptly to tales of his father "coming up and how he played from the minor leagues to being at the big league level. I use him as a tool and I try to take everything I can out of him and the knowledge he has."

Michael sees an edge in being able to use his father "as a tutor and a mentor all at the same time. On and off the field. Just everything that has to do with baseball, he's already been through it. So it's just beneficial for me to go to [my father]."

He added some of what was handed down to him were things the average fan might not think of, such as feeling more comfortable in the clubhouse than a player who had no idea what a big league clubhouse would be like. "Just growing up in a clubhouse watching guys your whole life and how they act and how they handle [matters] and go about their business makes it easier for you—so you know what to do when you come up here. And it's not always just bright lights and [having to get] over the shock [of being there]." Brantley said he grew up watching peers of his father and realized he should "try to follow in their footsteps."

Many fathers who played in the majors pass information on to their children beyond the how-to's of baseball. "That's one-hundred percent true," said Michael of his situation. "When I was on the trading rumors I talked to him about, 'Hey, what happened, what's going to happen, how am I to act?' He just kept me levelheaded throughout the whole thing."

Michael says no matter what questions he pitches his father's way, an answer is quickly forthcoming: "He almost knows *every* answer." And that ranges from the politics of baseball, to how to treat fans and the media, to the money matters of the game—the entire gamut of what big leaguers go through.

One thing Mickey didn't have to tell his son about was life in the minors, and that's because he *showed* him what that was like, exposing him to the lower levels of pro ball when he was a roving hitting coordinator with the New York Mets and Michael was a young boy. Michael explains, "When I didn't have school, I'd pick out at least two or three trips a year that he would take me on."

Usually they chose destinations that Mickey felt most comfortable with, treks which tended to be not too far from home. Still, as Michael said, "I've been through all the bus trips. I have been on all the long ones, all of the stops. I traveled with the team and was the batboy sometimes. I just enjoyed being in the minor league locker room with him. I was fortunate enough to be around a whole bunch of great athletes. I learned from them, watching what they did."

Michael told sportswriter Paul Hoynes of *The Plain Dealer*, "I really don't have one great memory, I have tons. From the Mets, to the Blue Jays [where Mickey was a hitting coach], even in the minor leagues taking the team buses. I embraced it because I didn't always get to see him because he was working so hard."

His trips with dad took him to teams with ports of call such as St. Lucie, Florida, and Burlington, Iowa, and Michael considers his travels to have been a great learning experience: "I couldn't thank him enough for at least giving me time and the opportunity to be in a minor league clubhouse at ten, eleven years old, and getting the work in that I needed to play baseball. Ever since I was [very young] I've been in minor and major league locker rooms each and every year. It was a privilege and an honor to just shake some hands with the guys that I met—you meet so many great people."

Mickey made sure he brought his son along on his trips whenever possible because his job required constant travel and thus a great deal of absence from family. Michael noted, "In order to spend more time and [have] opportunities with him and baseball in that period of his life, I went on road trips with him. I loved doing it so it was exciting for both of us."

In addition, his father entertained him along the way. "We just tell different stories—weather conditions or things that we did on the bus to keep it fun—little stuff like that."

Make no mistake, players do have to come up with ways from going berserk on bus trips. Even though minor league travel conditions are better nowadays than they were in Mickey's day, Michael noted, "It's basically the same, and life in the minor leagues is not fun. You go bus to bus, city to city. The PB and J's [peanut butter and jelly sandwiches], you get sick of them. In the offseason you never eat them because you know in season you're going to get them almost every day. It's tough sometimes but it's all worth it once you get to the major league level."

Michael's playing days actually began at a very young age. As Michael tells it, "I started at the age of four—I started at T-ball. At nine years old I was actually in "A" league which was nine-through-twelve, and there were some big guys at twelve years old, and I'm only nine. I was the littlest one on the team. I was playing pretty well and my dad said, 'Hey, you can kind of handle it up there, huh?' I was like, 'I guess so.' So that was kind of the year where I kind of opened my eyes and said, 'Hey, I'm a pretty good player.' And I just kept playing from there on."

Playing in a league with such a wide disparity in ages could have been daunting and, in fact, that youth league has now changed their age brackets. Michael explains, "That helps everybody out because, [when you're] nine years old and you see a twelve-year-old out there on the mound, it's a little intimidating." Actually, in retrospect, playing in the league and going up against the big boys was probably highly beneficial for Michael. A sports theory held by tennis players, among others, states you never get better by playing against others who aren't as good as you—you only improve by playing against opponents who are better than you are.

Having a supportive father like Mickey allowed Michael, many years later, to smoothly handle more serious adversity: being traded at the age of twenty-one. Michael was swapped from the Milwaukee Brewers to Cleveland along with Matt LaPorta and two other players for the Indians ace pitcher CC Sabathia.

While many fans may not realize it, players accept the fact that being traded is a part of baseball, but they often don't like it—being uprooted from one's home can be traumatic. Michael agreed, "It does affect you because you grow up with a locker room full of guys that you've been playing with at almost every level. It's sad to say, 'I got to go.' The team is going this way and I'm going that way now, but I still keep in touch with all the guys. You just have to stay levelheaded—it's difficult to not think about it, but at the same time you've just got to play baseball and whatever happens, happens."

Michael was able to maintain a degree of equanimity because, as he said, "My dad just told me to go out there and play [with your new team] again. Have fun no matter what. If you get traded tomorrow, then so be it, but at the same time enjoy your last days with your teammates. . . . So don't change the person that you are, stay within yourself and just have fun."

Mickey was also wise enough to offer solid advice about contract negotiations without becoming a sort of informal agent for his son. "He told me I'm not going to call anybody or say anything," recalled Michael. "He wanted me to do 100 percent on my own. Everything I kind of went through . . . if I had any questions about anything, I asked him, but at the same time [there] really weren't any big questions. He wanted me to pick out my agent because he said at the end of the day they work for you and I have to be comfortable with them making decisions for me—and the guy that I felt most comfortable with [is the one] I should choose."

Mickey's handling of the situation was far better than that of the father of former big leaguer Joe Dugan who once accepted, with dad's blessings, a contract for $500 to play pro ball, way back when that was pretty good money. Dugan said, "My father looked at the check and then told the scout, 'Throw in another hundred and you can take the rest of the family.'"

Michael said there was not a single life or baseball lesson taught to him by his father that sticks out—there were *many*. Michael explains, "I relied on him for so much, from driving to making decisions on buying a house now. It doesn't matter, I use him so much—just his knowledge. I just can't thank him enough for being with me."

His appreciation was perhaps never as strong as it was when he embarked on his big league career. Michael, the number seven draft pick of the Milwaukee Brewers in June of 2005, had accumulated a plethora of stickers on his suitcase, each with the name of a minor league whistle-stop in cities such as Helena, Montana; Charleston, West Virginia; and Huntsville, Alabama. Now, dues paid and having learned his trade in Milwaukee's chain, he was ready for the big time, but it took a change of scenery for him to earn his final step up the ladder to the majors.

The trade which sent him to the Indians led to his assignment to Columbus, Ohio, before Cleveland called him up and gave him his first start, a 2-for-2 showing on September 1, 2009. Clearly Michael had, through his process of osmosis with his father, soaked up the basics of the game and more, prompting a compliment from Cleveland general manager Mark Shapiro right after the Indians acquired Brantley. Shapiro noted that Brantley was "at an advanced level for his age." Given his background, that was understandable.

By July of 2010 Michael, due to his ability and an injury to Grady Sizemore, took over as the everyday center fielder for Cleveland. From August 30 to September nineteen, he was, like the dog days of the season, blazing hot. He strung together a nineteen-game hitting streak which was the longest by an Indians rookie since Hall of Famer Larry Doby hit in twenty-one straight contests back in 1948. Having hit .300 or better in nearly every one of his minor league stints, he came through with thirty-five hits in his twenty-eight games with the Indians.

By early 2011 it appeared as if Michael—in his third big league season and already sporting a .313 batting average from his rookie season— was ready to bloom. His manager with the Cleveland Indians, Manny Acta, stated, "I really trust Michael at the plate in any situation. He's going to be a pretty good hitter. He has all the intangibles to be a great player." Many of those intangibles can, of course, be traced to Mickey, who was with Seattle from 1986 through 1989 and hit a personal and team high of .302 in 1987.

Now, as an established big leaguer, Michael uses his offseasons to make up for lost time with his father. "We always have at least a two-week fishing period in the offseason where we take one of the campers that we bought. We go out there—just a little father and son time—we go fishing together. I look forward to that each and every year. That's one of my best experiences I could ever have, and hopefully one day when I have kids I could do the same as well."

As a high schooler Michael played both baseball and golf at Fort Pierce Central High in Florida. He was such a talented athlete he tried out for the golf team with no experience on the links. By the time he graduated he had become one of the best golfers on the squad as he "flipped flopped every now and then" between being the number one and the number two player there, pitted against the other squad's best golfers. Even now he says he shoots in the high 70s to low 80s.

Michael noted that he and his father "play golf all the time in the offseason," and while their bond is as tight as the skin of a kettle drum, they are both driven to outdo any opponent when they hit the links. Competitive? Michael explains, "Oh, *very* competitive. He was a major leaguer; I'm a major leaguer right now—the competitiveness still comes out. I give him a couple of strokes here and there to make it a little bit challenging. He hasn't beaten me in a long time, but he keeps talking like he is." Typical father and son.

Adam LaRoche

Photo Courtesy of Dave LaRoche

A dam LaRoche goes by his middle name, but he was named Dave after his father. Not so long ago he did something which had to have made his namesake proud—he overcame his Attention Deficit Disorder (ADD) which he was diagnosed with in high school.

Fortunately, his case was not extremely severe and he was able, at first, to fight through the problems that his condition entailed. He confessed that his ADD caused him at times to forget the count or the number of outs. He once caught a ball at first base for an out, then, thinking it was the final out of the inning, he jogged toward the dugout. Other times he'd record the third out and begin to lob the ball around the horn. He joked that while teammates get on him about such moments, he had found a bright side to the issue: "When I screw up, I've got an excuse."

However, Adam's problem was serious enough that it could have feasibly curtailed or perhaps even ruined his baseball career. As a child he told his mother and father that he sensed something was wrong and that, due to his "outward signs," he wondered if he should seek the help of a doctor. Some signs came early and were displayed on youth baseball diamonds when he would commit glaring blunders on the base paths. Although he was able to earn decent grades in class, his parents mused that he might be seeking an excuse not to do his homework. "His nature was so laid back," Dave commented. "You didn't know if he was daydreaming or thinking or just being stubborn."

Although Adam did try medication when he played winter ball in Puerto Rico early in the 2000s to help control his ADD, he did not like the side effects of the treatment and stopped taking the drug. Then, around the middle of the 2006 season, when he was with the Braves, he began taking Ritalin. He had come to realize that he simply had to combat his problem due to increasing mistakes on the field. For example, one time a portion of a broken bat and a ground ball both came in his direction at first base. Adam inexplicably fielded the bat, and not the grounder.

As a matter of fact, Adam can pinpoint the one play which vividly brought his situation to light, and perhaps even made him rethink the taking of improved medications. In May of 2006 he gathered in an easy ground ball which would have been turned into the final out of the inning, but he relaxed so much Washington's Nick Johnson beat the play out and the Nationals went on to score four unearned runs in an 8-1 win over Atlanta. This time he refused to blame his misplay on his condition, taking what was called "an admirable stance."

Adam has since settled in and has enjoyed a solid career. He drove in a personal high 100 runs in 2010 and, through 2011, had 164 homers to his credit.

If someone would have told Dave (who pitched fourteen years in the majors and reportedly never earned a salary of more than six digits) that there would come a time when his son—when *any* player, for that matter—would earn $15 million for playing two seasons in the majors, he would have scoffed. But that's exactly what Adam signed for prior to the 2011 season.

Perhaps, though, given the amount of hard work they put in together when Adam was young, Dave might not have been so taken aback. Young Adam's routine consisted of gulping down a breakfast then gathering up his equipment and tracking down his father before heading out to their backyard batting cage back in Kansas. That routine remained steady even during the days of "an early-winter frost." Adam recalled, "We'd be out there for hours and hours."

Those lengthy sessions were often punctuated by breaks due not to the usual reasons such as rain or fatigue, but to a rule instituted by Dave. As a crafty pitcher he realized that sometimes a batter gets himself out. That is to say, if a hitter chases a bad pitch, becomes overanxious, or tries to pull balls which should either be taken for a ball or possibly punched to the opposite field, then it wasn't so much the talent of the pitcher that retired him, but the hitter's own foolish mistake. This was a lesson Dave felt compelled to pass on to Adam.

After all, Dave had become famous for throwing a pitch which was much like the eephus (a baseball term which may come from a Hebrew word meaning "nothing") pitch of Rip Sewell who himself gained fame for rainbowing the pitch to Ted Williams in an All-Star game. Williams whiffed on the first blooper then asked Sewell to challenge him with another. When Sewell obliged, Williams deposited the extreme changeup into the bullpen.

LaRoche named his pitch the La Lob. Call it what you want, but the rare gimmick pitch floated as much as twenty feet off the ground in a baseball version of comic relief. Dave, a two-time All-Star, used his tricky pitch along with his standard ones to compile 126 saves

With that in mind, Dave told his son that anytime he pulled the ball when he threw him batting practice, the session was done. "He'd quit," said Adam. "He'd say, 'Pick up the balls, we're going inside.'"

It seems the temptation to rip the ball for power was too great for Adam to resist so their sessions continued to be on-again, off-again in nature. Dave remembered their minor disputes: "We'd come back inside in ten minutes. We would get into it a little bit, because I wanted him to use the whole field. In about a half-hour, everything would cool down and we'd get back out there."

When Adam got off to a poor start in 2007 with the Pirates—reverting to bad habits, over swinging and becoming pull happy, thereby disregarding dad's advice—it was as if Adam, wrote Rob Biertempfel, "half-expected his dad to emerge from the box seats at PNC Park and once again pull him off the field for a timeout." Adam put it another way, chuckling, "I'm sure he wanted to reach through the TV and do that a lot of times."

Adam, incidentally, has no memories of his father's pitching because he was only around two years old when Dave finished his playing days. Still, he has heard about his father's feats from coaches. "What I remember about his career was his coaching [for the Chicago White Sox and the New York Mets] when he was done playing." By that time Adam was old enough for Dave to take him along to spring training, an experience he has never forgotten. In addition, Adam traveled with his father's club at times and, like many sons of big leaguers, served as a batboy and hung out in the clubhouse, learning a great deal about baseball and its players.

Despite that background and despite being from a family with a strong athletic bloodline, Adam was not drafted until the twenty-ninth round of the 2000 draft. His father noted that Adam's case was unusual in that "all the teams wanted him as a pitcher. He told them he wanted to see if he could hit first. He was even asked if [he would re-consider] if he was drafted in the first round. 'For $2 million? What price would it take?' He said it has nothing to do with money. He wanted to play everyday." Only the Braves agreed to his terms.

Adam believes his lack of speed (and his thin physique) prevented him from being drafted higher. He theorized big league clubs tend to covet kids who possess an easy-to-spot attribute such as speed or power, and they can justify the investment they make in those players, pointing to their salient skills.

Adam hardly made the Braves organization rethink their decision to draft him so low by the time he spent his first full season in the minors at Myrtle Beach in 2001. Even Adam called the year "terrible," and said his .251 batting average attested to the fact that "I just couldn't figure it out." The following season his resiliency was astonishing and he piled up 72 RBI.

Adam's big league debut came in 2004 and he worked tirelessly, struggling to become an established player with the Braves, despite the

Photo Courtesy of Dave LaRoche

fact that he had become the first rookie in National League history to get his first two big league hits in the same inning. He called the feeling he got when he collected his initial two hits a dream-like one. As a kid Adam had fantasized about such moments: "When it happens, you don't actually believe it's happening. It's a weird feeling. I couldn't feel my legs for my first three or four innings of that game." Of course he added that getting those hits had special importance because his father and family were in attendance that day.

Back then he commented that the "toughest thing in the game is hitting. Your defense can be consistent—there's no excuse to screw up on defense—but hitting is going to come and go. It's been a little tough not playing everyday so you sit for a couple of days then come out and hit. So I'm still trying to get used to that, get used to the platooning role." LaRoche, like many other players who were stars in, say, high school, college, and the minors, was not accustomed to having to share a position on the field and, therefore, being required to share at bats. His father had led him to understand just how tough it is to break into the majors. So, like other young players who were overjoyed to find themselves in the big leagues, Adam added, "I can't complain."

He certainly had no complaints when, given the opportunity to play in vital postseason games, he made his family proud, producing a game-tying double and a game-tying home run during Atlanta's two victories in the 2004 National League Division Series versus the Houston Astros. His future looked golden and he remembered how his childhood goal had been not simply to follow his father's path into the majors, but to make it all the way to the Hall of Fame.

By 2006 he said he finally felt as if he belonged in the Bigs, that he was an established veteran, a leader—comments that made his father smile. Adam had gained the confidence and the comfort required to settle in. Just the year before, he had swatted more homers by the end of July than he had hit for the entire 2004 season: thirteen. He attributed much of his performance "to growing up around the game."

It was between the end of the 2007 season and the start of the next spring training camp, that Adam and a coach spotted a mechanical flaw pertaining to LaRoche's hips. He changed his offseason workouts as he went back into the cage he owned in his Fort Scott, Kansas, home—this one a "heated, well-lit indoor batting cage." It was there that, yet again, his dad threw batting practice to him, again admonishing him to take good cuts and to spray the ball to all fields. As always Adam found his father's insight and advice to be invaluable: "He knows my swing better than anybody. I've had this same swing my whole life. So if there are some problems, he'll pick it up."

At times the two would just toss the ball around and talk baseball. Dave related, "What I told him was, it's not just, 'My swing's ready. I'm strong enough.'" It was a bit more complicated than that: Dave wanted his son to also prepare himself mentally. Dave knew, for example, that Adam loved to hunt for deer during offseasons so he noted, "Mentally, it takes him a little while to get out of his tree stand and into the batter's box." So Dave, then a minor league pitching coordinator for the Toronto Blue Jays, was there to help with all the facets of Adam's game. After all the assistance he provided to Adam, Dave was especially pleased when his son, normally a slow starter, homered in his first at bat during the 2008 exhibition season and went on to hit twenty-five home runs.

Another lesson Dave certainly got through to Adam was to be consistent. *Washington Post* writer Adam Kilgore said Adam "grew to most respect the players who never wavered. 'A bad day, you can't let it bother you,' Adam LaRoche heard his father tell his pitchers. 'A good day, it's not going to help you tomorrow.'" The net result: Adam refuses to sulk after a strikeout or become demonstrative after hitting a key home run.

Adam has also learned not to be concerned about things he has no control over such as people's perceptions of him. "I'm not going to change the type of person I am to satisfy critics," he stated, adding that strikeouts and losing do bother him but he simply tends to be somewhat stoical about such matters.

Thanks to his father's input and his own evolution as a hitter, Adam developed a routine by the time he had settled in as a Brave: "My pre-game thing is usually by myself—taking a couple of swings off the tee either before B.P. or right after B.P. I take a regular batting practice, but nothing extraordinary." He, of course, did his mental homework, too, "about thirty minutes of video on that night's pitcher before the game which is nice—you get to see what you're up against. And I usually talk with Chip [Chipper Jones] about the starting pitcher if he's faced him before, just to get a feel on how they pitch him from the left side."

In Atlanta LaRoche also found a sort of surrogate father (not as if Adam, with Dave for a dad, really needed one) in Braves manager Bobby Cox. It's tough being away from home for youngsters and major league rookies are no exception. As early as August of 2004, with fewer

than 100 games played in the majors, LaRoche already knew how special Cox was: "You can't help but be impressed [by him]. I haven't heard a bad thing about him. There's just nothing but raves about him. He really is a smart manager, a players' manager, and I haven't seen any negative sides—it's been awesome. From a personal standpoint, I haven't been doing great, I've been kind of holding my own, and he's still putting me in there against righties all the time.

That's pretty cool, keep running the young guys out there, letting them get their feet wet—a lot of patience. The guys just respect him so much that you just do the right thing. You want to win and play hard for him."

During a 2006 interview Adam told *USA Today Sports Weekly*'s Seth Livingstone that he had once harbored dreams of being a pitcher just like his father, and that he loved his younger days when he was on the mound. "I still miss pitching. In fact, I go down to our bullpen about every other week just to see if I've still got it." Having had his father as an unofficial coach, Adam had pitched in junior college for two years and had major league teams interested in his arm. However, by that point he had his heart set on playing first base and the Braves were the only club willing to use him solely at that spot. Still, he did make it a point to tell Cox and the Atlanta coaching staff that in a pinch—say during a blowout—he wanted

Photo Courtesy of Dave LaRoche

to be placed atop the list of regulars who could take to the hill in a mop-up role. Like his father with his famed super slow pitch, Adam said that his out pitch would be his change-up.

Dave's son Andy (four years younger than Adam) is an infielder, primarily a third baseman, who was considered to be a top prospect due to, among other things, his strong arm—perhaps inherited from Dad? In 2005 he put up glittering stats with the bat, leading the entire Los Angeles minor league system in home runs and runs driven in. Through 2011 he had spent five seasons in the majors.

Another son, Jeff, Dave's oldest child, a year-and-a-half older than Adam, spent time in professional baseball, too. Drafted by the Pirates in 1997, he wound up pitching in the minors from 1998-2002 and in 2004 before concluding his career overseas in Holland as a player/manager.

Adam and Andy had the opportunity to meet on a big league diamond in a spring training game back on March 3, 2006, when Andy suited up for the Dodgers to face the Braves. During batting practice Andy's teammates goaded him to show up his brother. Likewise, when Adam took his pre-game cuts, the Braves teased him to outdo his younger sibling. During the game after Andy singled he was congratulated at first base by his coach and then by his brother in a moment bound to make a father elated. It was also a moment which afforded Adam the opportunity to take a verbal jab at his little brother. He stated he wished Andy would have doubled instead of singled. His motive was hardly one of brotherly love—he quipped that he had hoped for an apparent extra base hit so he would have had the opportunity to tackle Andy, holding him to a single.

It wasn't until August 14, 2008 before the two of them, who had played in so many casual games as kids, appeared together as teammates in a major league contest—a full two weeks after the Pirates had acquired the twenty-four-year-old Andy to join Adam, then in his second year with Pittsburgh. The brothers had never before been on the same team together, not counting pick-up games, of course. Growing up they never played on, say, the same Little League team for one simple reason: "He's always been just a little bit too young," said Adam.

So, when Adam came off the disabled list and was inserted into the Pittsburgh lineup with his brother, it was a great moment for the LaRoche family. Adam observed, "Finally, we're both healthy and can play together. This is what we've been looking forward to. We've been talking about this day. It's pretty neat." The brothers even batted back-to-back with Adam hitting cleanup, handling duties at first base, and Andy in the number five slot in the order, playing across the diamond from his brother at the hot corner. Andy teased that he would give his brother's scooping and stretching prowess a trial with his throws: "I'm going to make him earn that paycheck. I'm going to throw it in the dirt, see what he's got and test him out. I'll get him."

Their father could instantly relate to their typical brotherly interaction and joking. He could also, at long last, watch his boys in action without having to switch channels or travel to two different cities.

Chipper Jones

Photo Courtesy of Lynne Jones

Chipper Jones truly is a chip off the old rugged and dependable
block, with that block being his father Larry. Actually Larry is really Larry Wayne, Sr. and Chipper is Larry, Jr. Chipper's mother,
Lynne, once remarked that her husband and son "are absolute clones."

Chipper was born in DeLand, Florida, and is an only child who truly
bears a striking resemblance to his dad . He said that Larry "is probably

my best friend on the planet. He and I are very close. We talk three or four times a week. Any time I needed to take batting practice or catch passes or shoot baskets—whatever I needed to do—he was always there helping me out. It's not just my dad, it's my mom too. They work in tandem. Everybody should be so lucky to have the same set of parents that I do."

Even into adulthood Chipper continued to make abundant time for his parents and made it a point to get together with dad to hunt and fish—with "together" being the key word.

As early as childhood, Chipper set baseball goals for himself (including wanting to become a major leaguer). Chipper was lucky enough to acquire some of his athletic ability from Larry who was drafted by the Chicago Cubs. Chipper recounted, "He was a shortstop at Stetson University—didn't sign—decided to get a job because a little one [Chipper] was on the way.

"My mom is a professional equestrienne so there's quite a bit of athleticism in our family. I couldn't beat my mom in arm wrestling until I was seventeen and, to this day, she can make huge animals stand at attention just by the little things that she does. She commands respect.

"In the equestrienne world, I liken her to somebody like Mark McGwire—you know, Big Mac walks into the batting cage, everybody in the stadium stops and watches what he's doing—that's my mom, that's the kind of respect that my mom garners whenever she rides into the ring." Of course, the interview in which he made these statements was conducted prior to the baseball steroid scandal implicating McGwire, but his point about respect for Lynne remains.

"Both my grandfathers were athletes; not professional athletes," Chipper stated, "but it's just in the blood. We're a very active family and it just seemed like sports was kinda' bred into me." He added that while he did play football as a kid, his was definitely "a baseball family, so baseball wasn't taken too lightly." It was the one topic that dominated most of the conversation between Chipper and Dad.

Chipper, a self-proclaimed perfectionist who sports a near-perpetual smile, always had a strong work ethic and a drive to excel, qualities which Larry said did more for Chipper "than his natural ability." He also pointed out that Chipper "will compete with you in dominoes, Scrabble, and gin rummy, just like he's playing the seventh game of the World Series."

Bobby Cox, who managed Jones for an eon, said Chipper always was concerned with what was best for the Braves as a team, not for himself and said that quality came from his family—"good people."

In a chapter from the book *Chipper Jones: A Brave Legend in the Making*, Larry stated that Chipper first displayed an interest in baseball when he was just three years old back when Larry was a high school coach and Chipper wanted to tag along with dad to the field on a daily basis. Too active to sit idly, he was as fidgety as a fitful insomniac—that is until some of Larry's players agreed to pitch to and play catch with him.

Back home Larry painted a strike zone on the back of a garage located at the horse farm where Lynne taught dressage. Larry pitched tennis balls to Chipper for their numerous batting practice sessions.

From there it was on to his days playing organized baseball in a " minor league" where Chipper pitched and played shortstop when he

Photo Courtesy of AP Images

was six. By the time he reached high school his fastballs hit the high 80s and he added the outfield position to his resume when he was in Legion ball. When not on a youth team's diamond, Chipper hit against Larry who would launch fastballs, albeit using tennis balls from a distance of forty feet. Using a lightweight piece of PVC pipe for a bat at first, he attributed his workouts with dad as the reason he became a great fastball hitter.

Larry also helped his son learn how to hit both ways, preaching the value of that skill and using Mickey Mantle, his boyhood hero, as a paradigm of switch-hitting. When Larry was around ten years old he once served as a batboy in a spring training game between the Tigers and Mantle's Yankees. Decades later when Chipper was compared favorably to Mantle, Larry stated such an assessment was "beyond what I could have ever hoped for or thought would ever happen to my son." Plus, the fact that Chipper "embraced that comparison," continued Larry, "it thrills me to no end. It kind of brings tears to my eyes, to be honest with you." If Chipper maintains his career .300+ batting average he will accomplish something no switch-hitter ever achieved—a .300 average with 400+ homers.

Larry's key switch-hitting sermon concerned the necessity to work at staying sharp from both sides of the plate. He also stressed a quick, short stroke and staying behind the ball. Despite delivering such messages from his baseball pulpit, Larry insists that Chipper, a natural righty, pretty much learned the art of switch-hitting on his own. Father and son sat together watching the Game of the Week on TV faithfully. "Then," Larry remembered, "we'd go outside and imitate the game. If a left-handed hitter came up, you'd have to hit left-handed. I remember Chipper imitating [switch-hitter] Reggie Smith . . . He'd imitate his various stances—I used to laugh at him like crazy."

When Chipper was twelve, a year after Larry conceded to his wife that he could no longer blow fastballs by his son, the budding star starched three home runs in a game against Altamonte Springs and went on to compete in the finals of the Little League World Series. After that eye-popping showing Larry told his wife that he believed Chipper was among the top ten kids in his age bracket in the nation. Lynne gently chided him, "Yeah, right, you're just a Little League dad." Not all that many years later Larry would jokingly gloat, "I told you so."

Two years later, while only in eighth grade, Chipper was playing second base on his high school's varsity team, going up against young men who were up to four years older than him.

Even with beaucoup baseball savvy, Larry made it a point not to coach Chipper formally. When Chipper was ready to go out for the Taylor varsity baseball team, Larry, then a coach at that school, informed his boss that he didn't like the idea of coaching Chipper. "I believe dads should not be on the competitive field with their sons," he declared. With that credo in place, Chipper went to The Bolles School after his freshman year at Taylor. A private boarding school located in Jacksonville, Bolles was roughly ninety miles away from the Jones home. Chipper stayed at his new school during the week and returned home on weekends. "I didn't want to put too much pressure on him and didn't want people to think I catered to him," said Larry of the move to pull his son from Taylor.

Perhaps the main reason for the transfer was that Chipper was getting A's and B's at Taylor without so much as glancing at a textbook at home. "He was catching some breaks at Taylor," stated Larry, speculating that it could have been due to the fact that he worked there or because Chipper was a standout athlete. In either case he decided that just wasn't going to fly.

The transition wasn't easy at first. When Chipper initially called home complaining about his new school and his poor grades there, Larry was blunt with his son because he felt "that if you let your kids quit once, it would be easier to quit the second time. I told him, 'Coming home is not an option.'" Soon Chipper's grade point average rose to 3.2 (of a possible 4.0) and things were fine. Lesson learned.

Call it kismet, but the following three seasons he and his new teammates took on Pierson High in the state playoffs; Bolles prevailed each time. Overall, Chipper's team went 66-19 over his three-year stretch and they advanced to the state finals twice, winning it all on one occasion.

That took place when Chipper, a junior, won all five of the games which took his squad through the state title game. After winning the championship game he trotted over to the stands and embraced his father.

In 1990 Chipper, playing short and pitching, hit .488 as a senior and posted a 7-2 record with a nifty 1.00 ERA on the mound. He also was a first-team All-State football player, skilled enough to earn scholarship offers from football powerhouses such as USC.

When the Braves selected Chipper as the highest overall pick in the draft, Larry served as his son's negotiator. A compromise between the two parties earned Chipper a $350,000 signing bonus, then a record for a high schooler.

Larry passed on other words of wisdom to his young son. A believer, as he once wrote, that a child "will give you what you demand of them," he firmly but lovingly raised his son to strive to always do his best. Chipper, suitably schooled, refused to be mediocre.

In 1992, the year before Chipper's big league debut, he attended a card show and met Mantle who, wrote Terrence Moore, "shared stories and gave advice to his nervous visitor." Mindful of his father's admiration of Mantle, Chipper got an autographed baseball and later presented it to Larry.

In Chipper's rookie season, 1995, the Braves defeated the Cincinnati Reds allowing them to advance to the World Series. After knocking off the Reds, Chipper shared his elation and a Kodak moment with his father, exiting the clubhouse and rushing over to Larry, whispering in his ear, "Dad! Can you believe I'm going to play in a World Series. It's just like a dream." A dream best shared with loved ones, especially after the Braves won it all, defeating the Indians.

Chipper could relate to the bond between other fathers and sons. He smiled, for example, reminiscing about playing "against Griffey, Jr. my whole career, and I got a chance to have his father as a hitting coach in the World Baseball Classic. That was a lot of fun, just being able to soak

Photo Courtesy of Lynne Jones

up as much as possible from some great bloodlines. It was a treat. It was a blast—probably my most favorite baseball moment."

In 2009, Chipper, his swing as quick and as smooth as flowing mercury, won the NL MVP. He was catapulted to the award by a stretch during which he hoisted the Braves onto his shoulders and took charge, basically promising teammates, "Jump on my back, boys, and I'll carry us into the postseason." In a crucial late season, three-game series against the Mets who were duking it out with Atlanta for the division title, Chipper left the New York crew "chipwrecked," drilling four home runs in a sweep. In all, he played in the postseason eleven times, from his first full season (1995) through 2005.

In a 2010 interview with writer Steve Hummer, Chipper was as open as ever about his devotion to dad, saying he realized that, at the age of thirty-eight, he was perceived as an old-timer. However, he noted that in his parents' eyes, "I'm always going to be the ten-year-old kid who used to get his butt whipped every day because he was bad. The one who told a little white lie or stole cookies out of the cupboard. . . ." Larry, who Chipper called a tough love kind of parent, echoed those sentiments: "He is still my son playing a game." Further, Larry expressed his excitement for "where he's [Chipper] at and the career he has had. But I don't care how old they get; they're still your little boy."

Going into 2011 Chipper's career seemed to be in jeopardy, with him having to fight through a torn anterior cruciate ligament in his left knee late the previous season—he even considered retirement. Chipper recalled his father having once told him not to make such a decision when he was either too emotionally high or low. He plugged away.

Still, the prospect of leaving the game saddened the entire Jones family. His parents stated that they dreaded the day Chipper would hang up his cleats for good, but at one point in 2010 they said they were prepared to accept it being his final season. "I'm good with the fact that the end is near," Larry told the *Atlanta Journal-Constitution*. "I'm going to miss coming to the ballpark. I just hope the end comes with him playing well. I hate for him to walk away from it and feel like he was on the down slope." Lynne, whose son was struggling, hitting .233 at the time of the interview, said that no matter what the case may be "we're going to shed tears."

Larry also observed there was "nothing nicer than flipping on the TV every day and seeing your son there." Chipper added that when he does retire he fully understands how tough it would be on his father. "It will be like losing me all over again, like when I went away to high school," he said.

The tears were put on hold, though, as Chipper was not about to depart on the "down slope." Instead, he got off to a fine start as the new season rolled around. On April 26, 2011, the veteran third baseman drove in three runs, pushing him into sole proprietorship of the number two slot on the all-time list of RBI by a switch-hitter, (1,512). He breezed by Mickey Mantle (1,509) and trails only Eddie Murray (1,917).

Chipper said passing Mantle was something special: "He [Mantle] was my dad's guy and the reason he made me a switch-hitter." Jones continued, "I grew up in the shadow of Mickey Mantle my whole youth and I could sense that [my dad] and mom were welling up last night when I tied him. So I can't imagine what it was like today."

After the games in which he tied and surpassed Mantle's total, Jones received text messages from his parents who were unable to attend the contests. They sent their love and congratulations. Chipper also commented, "It's gratifying. I look at the numbers as me just going out and doing my job. That's the way I've always approached it. I've never really thought about my place or anything like that. But when you grew up hearing about Mickey the way I did and with the reverence that I did from my father, to pass him in career RBIs is quite a feat." Larry marveled at how he was able to now utter, "The Chip and The Mick in the same sentence."

Another personal highlight of 2011 came on June 10 when the Braves traveled to Houston to take on the Astros. Jones led his team to an 11-4 win, going 3-for-5 including his sixth homer. In a post-game interview Chipper, who hadn't exactly been stinging the ball in recent games, said that he always greatly anticipated playing in Houston because it was the venue which his parents could easily reach to watch him play in person and to offer him advice. His folks live on and run a sprawling, 10,000-acre farm in Carrizo Springs located in southwest Texas which they dubbed Double Dime Ranch in honor of the jersey number (10) worn by Larry during his school days and by Chipper at many levels of play up into the Bigs.

Chipper, agreeing with the "father knows best" line, has relied upon Larry as an unofficial hitting coach and often points out that nobody in the world knows his swing better than dad. Remembering the myriad times Larry offered a tip which straightened his batting out, Chipper again took heed of dad's pre-game suggestion before that June 10 game. Dad's input helped Chipper get two hits to the opposite field—a key, Chipper said, to effective hitting for him. Over the years dad had also offered instructional help in numerous ways such as sending Chipper videotape of him hitting, contrasting poor at bats with the ones he needed to emulate in order to get back in the groove.

The collective effort had paid off once again in 2011 when Chipper was named to the All-Star team, raising his total All-Star selections to seven. Career-wise, he and his parents could proudly look back at his laudatory feats. He rattled off a stretch of eight consecutive years with

100+ RBI, led his league in hitting (.364 in 2008), and, through 2011, owned a career .304 batting average with 454 homers, thirty-third all-time and number three for a switch-hitter.

When it came time for Chipper to name two of his children with his wife Sharon, he tied in his devotion to dad with his love for baseball, going with the names Larry Wayne III, or Trey, to honor his father, then Shea, named because of all of the success Chipper had while playing against the New York Mets in their old ballpark, Shea Stadium. "I love playing there. Check the numbers," he stated. Up to the date of Shea's birth Chipper had belted more homers in Shea Stadium than any other park on the road. His first big league home run also came there and he wound up hitting almost one home run for every four games he played there. Chipper and Sharon said that they were going to go with the name Shea regardless of whether it was a boy or a girl.

In one of his last trips to New York, Chipper requested a souvenir from the stadium (preferably a sign with the name Shea on it and/or a seat with Chipper's jersey number 10 on it) so he could place it in his son's room. He later purchased two orange seats from the ballpark for his son who, though not even five years old, was, according to Chipper, already hitting with authority. "He rakes," said a proud Chipper of Shea, who he labeled "a stud."

That Shea can stroke the ball is no surprise given who mentors him. Chipper instructed his sons, emphasizing an early lesson he gleaned from his father: never be afraid of the baseball.

Writer James Joyner quipped of Chipper's naming of Shea, "I'm just glad he didn't have his best outings at one of the stadia named after a corporation. 'Qualcomm Jones' just doesn't have a very good ring to it."

One story, perhaps more than any other, reveals a great deal about Chipper's respect for his father. Larry began the tale by noting Chipper's teammates call his son Larry. When Atlanta ace Greg Maddux played golf in a foursome with the Jones men, they approached the first tee and Maddux, realizing he was with two men named Larry, asked what he should call them. Chipper quickly replied, "Call me Chipper. This is Larry."

Jeff Francoeur

Photo Courtesy of AP Images

Jeff Francoeur (the family name translates as "French heart") was born in Atlanta in 1984 to Karen and Dave, workers in the education field. The family lived in Lilburn, Georgia, about one-half hour away from the Braves home park. Coincidentally, so did the family of Jeff's friend Brian McCann. Years later they attained their childhood dream when they became members of the Atlanta Braves.

Jeff's first memory involving baseball and his dad, a very faint memory, was the "first Braves game I ever went to [when] I was about to turn three. My dad took me to see the Bob Horner four home run game. It was cool." In 1991 as a second grader he was thrilled all season as Atlanta rolled along, making it to the World Series. His childhood bedroom was decorated with a poster of pitcher John Smoltz.

Jeff would go on to pitch and play center field for Parkview High School where he was a quarterback and an All-Star safety. His Panthers won state titles in his junior and senior seasons.

On high school baseball diamonds he hit .500 with twenty homers as a junior. His nationally-ranked ninth squad went 32-4 and won the state 5-A championship and he was a second-team All-American selection. As a senior he hit .487 and ended his Panther days with fifty-five home runs and another championship. This time, his sixth inning go-ahead homer, his grand slam later that same inning, and his relief stint on the hill, secured the title. Shortly after, he turned down a two-sport scholarship from Clemson and became a professional baseball player after being a first round draft pick by *his* team, the Braves, in 2002.

Jeff's path to the majors featured stops in Rome, Georgia; Myrtle Beach, South Carolina; Greenville, South Carolina; and Jackson, Mississippi; but by mid-season in 2005 he got the notification he had been waiting for—he was to make the jump to the major leagues. Jeff made his debut on July 7, 2005, and made it a very memorable one at that, a sort of belated fireworks display for the Francoeurs: "I know when I got called up to the big leagues and hit that home run in my first game, there was no one more excited than my dad because he [normally] never cheered real loud, he just kind of sits in his seat very quietly." This time things were different, though. Jeff watched replays showing "my dad putting his hands up and going crazy—that meant the world to me. I knew he was proud." Jeff calls that occasion "probably the greatest memory for me."

Jeff's rookie success was a blessing to his maternal grandfather, Melvin ("Pops" to Jeff). He had lost his wife before Jeff made it to the majors and was living in a nursing home, but each time Jeff played, Pops was infused with vitality, and his radio and television were his conduits to his grandson.

Jeff, known to teammates as "Frenchy," would soon add many more great accomplishments to make his grandfather (and father) applaud. In 2006, his first full season in the Bigs, he propelled twenty-nine home runs, still a career high, and drove home 103 runs, all at the age of twenty-two. The most emotional game of the year occurred in June, hours after Pops had passed away. That night Jeff crushed an extra-inning, walk-off homer. Teammates engulfed him at home plate and, shortly thereafter, Jeff dedicated the key blow to his grandfather.

The six foot two, 220 pound right fielder followed up his 2006 performance with 105 runs driven in the next season, and in 2011 he reached a personal high for doubles with forty-seven, second most in the majors.

A 2007 Gold Glove winner, Francoeur has a howitzer for an arm. On two occasions he has led his league in assists from the outfield, once with an astronomical nineteen. To put that statistic in perspective, nineteen assists is a season total bettered by legendary right fielder Roberto Clemente only twice in his career. Over his first six seasons no outfielder had more assists than Francoeur who, in 2011, threw out a position player at first base on what was seemingly a clean hit to the outfield. Testing his arm is a run-at-your-own-peril proposition.

On Father's Day of 2007 Jeff, then still a genial rising star outfielder with the Atlanta Braves, looked back over his childhood and spoke of how close he is with his dad: "On Father's Day we usually go to church then come home and play a big football game out in the backyard. My father'd be the all-time quarterback and my brother and I would go against each other all day.

"But you know, my dad, more importantly, has always supported me in what I did and he's always been a father first which has always been a big deal for me. I think too many times these days fathers are too much best friends with their kids instead of being a father and a disciplinarian. He was a principal for ten years and an assistant superintendent for about twenty, so he was a tough love type of guy, but obviously very encouraging, very helpful. He's always been that for me, he's always been a guy that's been straight-laced, very serious, but, at the same time I know through his actions that he loves me a lot."

Jeff, who calls his father his hero, recounted how Dave grew up in a very small house with a family who didn't possess a lot of money, and yet he went to Vanderbilt, got his degree, and built his own family. Jeff says of his father, "I'm always so proud because he works his butt off for what he gave our family. That means a lot. He raised us to know that school was coming first and everything [else] comes out second. He never wavered from that."

Jeff recalled the time "I lied about a test grade and my dad found out. I was in ninth grade playing J.V. football and he sat me out a whole game. The coach tried to convince my dad to let me play some, but I had to sit on the sidelines and watch the whole game; my dad wouldn't let me play. It was academics and family first. If I didn't do that, I wasn't going to play."

Baseball-wise, Dave combined having fun with learning. Jeff related, "When I was young my father and I used to set up bases in our playroom upstairs and he'd go over different force plays with me, and I wanted to know that stuff. That always meant a lot.

"He taught me to play the game. He taught me tough love. My dad never pushed me to do anything I didn't want to do, but I'll never forget T-ball. He knew I could hit off pitching—I didn't need the tee. There was one game when I was six years old where I missed four or five pitches and they asked if they could bring the tee out. My dad wouldn't let them. He said, 'You're hitting,' and he threw two pitches and I struck out. I went crying into the dugout and my dad said, 'You gotta' learn to hit.' I still say he threw hard on purpose so he could teach me that lesson. That always stuck with me because my dad expected me to do my best. He made me know what I needed to do."

When Jeff was a little older his family had "an old 1984 Caprice Classic and I remember we must have logged over 180,000 miles on that thing driving from Atlanta to Iowa, to Oklahoma, to play all those tournaments we did." Some years Dave coached Jeff and the other years he made sure he could attend Jeff's games faithfully, sometimes leaving work early to do so.

In every conceivable way Dave helped Jeff turn into a fine player *and* a fine human being. Jeff explains, "The first thing he is most proud of me is being a good husband, the morals and the things he instilled in me.

"I think the thing my dad did great that I think doesn't happen these days in parenting is this—all the way through high school and even my years in the minors, my dad was my dad first and my friend second. He had to be hard on me and make decisions and punish me when I'm sure he didn't want to, but he had to. I appreciate him for being that way. And now, he's my friend first. That's the great thing. We hang out, watch a game, and enjoy each other's company, enjoy hanging with each other."

Clearly Jeff feels he owes his dad a lot. "He knew it was my dream to be a big leaguer and if it wasn't for him I obviously wouldn't be here. He taught me everything. He knows my swing and tells me exactly what I'm doing."

Nowadays, Dave mainly sees Jeff on TV (no more long Caprice Classic trips) but, "A couple times a year he surprises me and flies into another city and we get to hang. That's the fun part—after the game. We won't talk about baseball—we'll go an hour-and-a-half just have a beer and just talk about life. The baseball stuff is good to him, but the way I've grown up and been able to handle some of my adversity, he's more proud of that."

While the Francoeurs certainly watched baseball together on TV as Jeff grew up, they loved to watch golf as well. When the British Open was on they'd begin their viewing day in the morning and watch it all day long. With that background, Jeff not only had baseball to help him bond with his dad, but golf, too, and they began a tradition of going on annual golf vacations as an excellent way to stay close and enjoy each other's company.

Both Jeff's father and brother D. J. played golf in college. "That's the first sport I played," Jeff recalled. "I was good at it, and I'm still good at it, I have a four handicap, *but* my attitude would get to me every once in awhile, so that's why I chose baseball—you can have a bad at bat, get pissed, and then be able to go back up, but in golf you've got to hold it together."

When Jeff became an established big leaguer, financially secure, he wanted to bestow a very special gift upon his father. A baseball outing wouldn't serve as a suitable present—too commonplace for this family — nor would it be much of a surprise. So Jeff turned to another father-son common denominator to show his appreciation to his father for all he had done over the years for his family.

Planning carefully, and keeping those plans secret for more than a year with CIA stealth, Jeff surprised Dave with a trip to Scotland in 2008 to shoot golf on several of the greatest courses anywhere on the globe, including St. Andrews. To this day they have a photo which shows father and son atop the famous Swilcan Bridge near the eighteenth fairway of St. Andrews' Old Course. Jeff wanted to reward those who had been there for him throughout his youth and into adulthood, and that included treating not only his father to the dream vacation, but D. J., an uncle, a brother-in-law, and two close family friends as well.

Their trip a rousing success, Jeff can look back to one especially tender moment when his dad put his arm around him and said, "When I'm on my death bed, I want you to remember this day because this is one of the greatest days of my life." Jeff commented, "My dad is not a very emotional guy. He's pretty tough. To hear that from him was really cool."

J. D. Drew

J. D. Drew grew up with parents David and Libby in a one-story brick house located in Hahira, a small town (population around 1,600) in the southern part of Georgia. His youth was a wholesome one, figuratively baked following a recipe consisting of a heap of family love, Christian faith, and diligence. Complete the recipe by liberally tossing in his three favorite sports: baseball, hunting, and fishing. He still says his hometown is the place where his roots are, and that despite seeing so much of the world, he has continued to love "the small-town life."

He and younger brothers Tim and Stephen, who also went on to become major leaguers, lived during a time period in which parents could transform into amateur video and still-picture biographers, capturing not only the usual "home movie" scenes such as birthdays and Christmas mornings, but every sports highlight ever turned in by their children. J. D. joked, his voice still carrying at least a trace of a Southern accent, that even though his parents were certainly good ones, there are very limited pictures of him and his brother. "My mom and dad were horrible about that," he said. Their memories are stored in their brains, not on film.

His father David wasn't entirely a baseball dad, either: "We were a football family growing up." While David wasn't very knowledgeable about baseball, he did support his kids and they tended to "play whatever was in season with pick up games in the yard with friends. I started playing baseball when I was twelve [the same time he informed his mother that he would become a major leaguer as an adult] and then after my dad saw it was something I liked doing, we started going to batting cages and stuff like that. So I would say [at] thirteen , fourteen years old we started kind of really focusing on playing baseball."

Around that same time J. D. made his own crude batting cage. He reportedly "used to staple gun [his mother's] good bedsheets to the back porch and hit balls into them." He took so much batting practice as he grew up, his hands became bloodied at times. Sheer drive and determination.

Still, he said his father was "pretty disappointed when I quit playing football after my ninth grade year—that's a big South Georgia sport. I think he thought baseball was just kind of a fad." David saw it as a sport in which players didn't have to wear pads and helmets under the scorching Georgia sun. However, baseball success soon came to J. D. and David not only recognized that, but as J. D. said, his support would have fallen into place "regardless."

One simple example of his father's support was his faithful appearances at Florida State to watch all of J. D.'s games. At FSU he became the first Division I player ever to hit thirty homers and swipe thirty bases in a single season. In 1997 the All-American hit a lusty .455 and collected 100+ hits, runs, and RBI, something only two other men ever accomplished.

J. D. noted that his father provided guidance for the entire family: "We grew up in church. He's a strong Christian. He's a strong believer and ultimately I think that's God's calling for a father and a family—to be the leader. No matter what you do financially—rich, poor, regardless—I think the important thing is to guide your family spiritually, and that's where he's really taught all of us really well."With that background it's obvious David is more satisfied by the fact that his son is a good person, than that he's a good ballplayer.

J. D. noted, "The biggest thing he [Dad] did growing up was work at [a company] building boats," but David has held down an assortment of jobs supporting his middle-class family.

He also had yet another important job—that of teaching his children right from wrong: "There was plenty of family discipline at our house. You know, with three brothers and Tim and I really close in age, we fought all the time, just little scraps and pestering each other. There's plenty of instruction in the Bible that [my father] heeded to and took into our family and made us better because of it."

Likewise, J. D. says that "me being a father, the proudest day of my life will be the day that my son makes that [spiritual] commitment over and above anything that he ever accomplishes in the work force."

With three sons who made it to the majors, the contentment David feels has to be immeasurable. "My dad's a hardworking man," continued J. D., "who never missed a day of work. Just continually pushing to better his family, give them the best that he could. So to watch us play every night, all over the country, I'm sure he's super excited about that. My dad's much more comfortable at home watching the games on TV

[now] than having to travel and sit in the stands where [he couldn't be] up close and personal. He's constantly watching."

Now that J. D. is an adult he has observed how some things have naturally changed since the days of his youth with his father. "I think everybody's relationship is going to be different. You move out of the house, you start your own family, they become grandparents and, you know, ultimately that's kind of the role everybody plays. He's getting to the point now where he's just enjoying his older age and watching his kids do their job and play. So it's a pretty special time for him."

The bottom line of the father-son relationship, the one thing which never alters, is the deep-rooted love which perpetually flourishes like crops in fertile Georgia soil. Additionally, even the strongest and most talented of major leaguers are unafraid to express that love. "Oh, yeah, we definitely, for sure, love our parents and I think that's the instrumental part," said J. D. You try to instill in your kids to respect the parents—that's what I do with my kids—and ultimately become not only their instructors but their friends and loving parents in the long scheme of things."

J. D. has other family members for fans. Tim said, "I look up to him more than anyone else on this earth." Tim said J. D. has always maintained a level head: "He knows it's not about him; it's about relationships with people one-on-one and his faith in Christ." He also praised his older brother for being a good man who works hard.

J. D. certainly learned the value of hard work and of a dollar early on. When he was just nine he worked during summers on his grandfather's farm from sunrise to sunset for $15 per day, driving a tractor, tending to livestock, and stripping tobacco. He told the *Atlanta Journal-Constitution*, "That taught me a lot about character and what life's about." His father added, "J. D. knows what it was to come up rough."

Stephen, three years younger than Tim and eight years younger than J. D., was the third of the three brothers to become first-round picks, an amazing feat. Like J. D., Stephen is a product of Florida State University who has some pop in his bat. Scouts liked his power, the ability to hit gap shots to all fields, and his soft hands and rifle arm at shortstop as well.

In his rookie season (2006) Stephen, then twenty-three years old, played against J. D. during a four-game set in July and picked up his first big league hit during that series against the Los Angeles Dodgers. Tim flew in to be on hand and other family members were also in attendance. J. D. told the *East Valley Tribune* of Mesa, Arizona, "The last time we played against each other there were ghost runners." That time period dated back to their days on sandlot fields in Georgia. They had clearly come a long way from those more casual games.

In 2007 when J. D. hit a grand slam in the sixth game of the American League Championship Series, he and Stephen became just the third set of brothers to connect for home runs in the same postseason. The other brother acts to achieve this rare feat were Clete and Ken Boyer, who did this in the 1964 World Series, and Robbie and Sandy Alomar Jr., who both connected in the 1997 postseason.

In cases in which both a father and son made it to the majors, the father almost unfailingly says he had hopes for his son to do better than he did. When a father, regardless of his occupation, has two or more sons who become professional baseball players, dad wishes for each and every one of them to succeed and put up stats similar to one another. Fathers don't want their sons to have even a single fleeting thought similar to that of comedian Tommy Smothers who joked about a parent preferring his brother over him. Big league dads don't want a son to wonder, "Maybe, just maybe, dad somehow relates more to my star brother than me." Therefore, such fathers recoil at the thought of having, say, one son becoming a star and another winding up as an up-for-just-a-cup-of-coffee type player—he truly wants the best for each offspring. That certainly is the case with David Drew, a man wise enough to judge people not by statistics, and more than warm enough to spread his love evenly among all of his children.

In the case of the Drew family, through 2011 J. D. has spent fourteen years in the majors, Stephen has been with the Arizona Diamondbacks since 2006, and Tim put in time in parts of five seasons in the majors. In May of 2011 he was attending Michigan State, studying physical therapy. Three success stories to be sure.

Barry Zito

Barry Zito's parents, Joe and Roberta, first met in an unusual way—unusual, that is, for most families, but perhaps not so peculiar for them. In 1961 they were both working for the singer Nat King Cole, and with music as their bonding agent, they fell in love. Barry's father actually composed music for Cole and also served as the conductor for his band while Roberta was a back-up singer in Cole's group, the Merry Young Souls. By the way, talent truly does run deep in this free-thinking family—Barry's uncle is actor Patrick Duffy, famous for portraying Bobby Ewing on the hit TV series *Dallas* which ran from 1978 through 1991.

Barry was born in (fittingly for a child of parents in the entertainment field) Las Vegas in 1978. He inherited not only his athletic talent but his musical skills as well—he is a fine singer and guitarist who learned the instrument on his own when he began fooling around with one in 2000 during his first spring training camp, back when he was with the Oakland A's. Quite serious about music, he had a recording studio built in his house, and, since those days when he first strummed on his guitar, he has added live performances with The Sally Zito Project, a group headed by his sister, and song-writing to his musical resume.

However, the most glistening item on his list of baseball accomplishments has to be the Cy Young Award, which he copped in 2002, just his second full season in the majors. That year he became the seventh youngest man to win the illustrious honor, winning decisions for Oakland at a dazzling .821 clip (23-5 with a tiny ERA of 2.75—his win total was the best in the American League and his ERA the third lowest). Incredibly, over a stretch from July 24, 2001, through the 2002 season he went 34-6, good for an ungodly .850 win-loss percentage with a 2.50 ERA—numbers that left fans agape.

Flash back to his childhood: Like so many men who wound up playing baseball for a living, the dream began at a very young age for Barry. Joe built a mound for his son in the backyard of their La Mesa, California, home when Barry was just seven years old. He immediately began pitching off that perch, already throwing what would become a vexing pitch to big league hitters (*Sports Illustrated* writer Ben Reiter called it a "nose-to-toes breaker") and learning a craft which would later earn him great pleasure and millions of dollars.

Speaking of the origin of his curve, Barry said he and his father "picked it up out of a book when I was seven. He caught me in the backyard." Later he would throw his pitches into a mattress, one that had the outline of the strike zone painted onto it. His commitment to baseball and his father's guidance paid off. Zito's curve, according to a 2005 poll of big leaguers, was the best in baseball, and an awestruck Alex Rodriguez said a hitter shouldn't even bother to sit on or look for a Zito curve because "you're not going to hit it."

Right after Barry won his Cy Young Award he grew retrospective, thinking back to his days as a boy when Joe and Roberta paid Randy Jones, who himself had won a Cy Young Award (1976 for the Padres), to give lessons to Barry, a fellow lefty. The weekly sessions, which the Zitos learned were being offered through an ad Jones had placed in a local newspaper, ran for around four years, starting when Barry was twelve. They cost $50 a pop, but were clearly well worth it.

Barry would complete workouts with his teams then trudge over to Jones' house for one-on-one instruction. "I was sitting there in his living room every day," said Zito, "and I would kind of marvel at it." After working outdoors with his pupils, Jones would invite only his top thirty-five students inside for skull sessions. Only the elite, the pitchers who displayed the most intense desire, gained admittance into the Jones inner sanctum of a living room.

Barry continued, "I remember vividly the four, five years we spent in the back yard with Randy. When I did something incorrectly, he'd spit tobacco juice on my shoes. Nike hightops we could barely afford, he's spitting tobacco juice on them."

When told of Zito's comments, Jones laughed, "I had to get his attention, and that worked with Barry." He recalled Barry as a student who didn't concentrate well initially but, "By the time he got into his teens, he locked in. He just kept getting better." Jones would stress to his top pupils, "Your goal is to be one of the two best pitchers in the world in any given year." Zito achieved that noble goal.

Barry, known for his assiduousness and preparation, said that after he won the pitchers' ultimate honor he had hopes of going on to win more Cy Young Awards. "My dad always told me 'Dream big and dream always.' It's not like I shoot for the Cy Young Award. I have big aspirations of what I want to do in this game and what I want to achieve in, hopefully, a long career." While he did not win the coveted award again, he would go on to make two All-Star squads after his monster season of 2002, making him a three-time All-Star.

The gifts his parents gave him, from those early lessons with Jones to the homemade mound and the battered mattress, were indicative of the type of people the Zitos were. Joe had, in fact, "basically quit music for eleven years to work with me," said Barry.

The loss of income which inevitably came with Joe out of work led to another sacrifice—the family moved to El Cajon, California, a less-than-lustrous town near the Mexican border. The family had to make do with the meager income Roberta earned as a minister. Sally Zito told *Sports Illustrated* that living in El Cajon was a terrible experience. "We lived in a 900-square foot home that apparently had been a halfway house for female prisoners. . . ." Constructed of steel, the structure was blazing hot in the summer and it squatted in a neighborhood in which sightings of police "helicopters circling" above were far from rare.

Shortly after Barry became a major leaguer, money would never again be an issue for him. When he left the Athletics via free agency and signed a seven-year deal with the San Francisco Giants in December of 2006, he must have felt like a just-struck-it-rich prospector when he agreed to the contract which called for the largest amount of money ever paid to a pitcher. By the time his pact with the Giants runs out he will have earned more than $130 million over his entire career, with the vast majority of that salary earned in a San Francisco uniform.

Barry, taught by his parents that believing in oneself can raise a person to nearly unimaginable heights, once said, "The only person who ever stops me from achieving something is me." Barry was pretty much echoing what his father told *Sports Illustrated* in 2004: "When you are focused and fixed in your desire, it doesn't really matter who the batter is, where you're playing or what the situation is." Joe went so far as to say that even if his son grooved a pitch right down the pipe, but did so with a pitch he was "committed to," the hitter would fail.

Making batters fail is something which doesn't come early in the careers of most pitchers, and early on in the majors Barry was no exception—things did not come so smoothly for him. He did post a fine rookie year in 2000 (7-4, 2.72 in fourteen starts), but by July of 2001 he certainly was not flashing a Cy Young form. His record stood at 6-7 and his inflated ERA was a shaky 5.01.

He immediately turned to his father, calling him and saying quite simply, "Something's wrong." Joe hopped a plane and in no time was in Oakland where he would spend five days trying to straighten out his son's mental slant on the game, stressing the power of positive thinking and avoiding negative ones. One must, Joe preached once more, believe in oneself. Joe's teachings were aligned more with philosophy than with pitching mechanics, but his lesson plan worked. The impact of the father-son tête-à-tête was as huge as it was instantaneous; Barry finished the season by going 11-1 with an invisible ERA of 1.32, a prelude to his upcoming Cy Young season.

Sadly, he has yet to match his 2002 season (although he did win sixteen games in 2006). Through 2011 he hasn't lived up to the big bucks the Giants forked over. His first season with San Francisco resulted in an 11-13 pitching slate. If that disappointed his fans, just try to fathom how they felt in 2008 when his record dipped to 10-17 with a 5.15 ERA. From 2007-2011 the Giants return on their investment was hardly glittering: Zito went 43-61.

Nevertheless, he was not about to turn tail and become a quitter. Joe didn't pass negative traits on to his son. During an interview for *Baseball Digest*, Barry reaffirmed that his father was the man who had influenced him the most as he was growing up, and that he did so in a very positive way: "He instilled in me to have a good work ethic and to always believe that I could do things with my life." Likewise, he said that the finest piece of advice he ever received also came from his father. "To sum it up," Barry recalled, "he said there's more inside of you that's powerful than what's outside of you."

Barry, observers said, always "remained true to himself and his character," even in the roughest of times, and one writer said Barry also typically lived up to his "California-cool image." Zito agreed that his life was still pretty simple. He preferred playing his guitar, surfing (being from southern California, taking up that hobby's almost a given), and dabbling in photography to the usual activities many players enjoy such as the vegetative act of watching TV. Zito once said he didn't even have cable in his home. Asked to name his favorite TV show, he replied that he didn't have one. All in all, even with his losing record as a Giant, Barry seemed unruffled on the mound as well as in life in general.

Perhaps, but in 2010 he candidly confessed that he felt as if he had "been through death and back," and that signing his enormous contract put a burden on him. "I found myself wanting to satisfy every fan, every San Franciscan. I wanted to really bring it home for the entire city. That's just too lofty of a goal." Reverting to his surfer roots, the somewhat Bohemian pitcher who once described himself as being "mellow and laid back," concluded, "One person can't do that. Dude, I learned the hard way."

In the *Baseball Digest* piece on Barry, he defined success on the baseball field as being consistent and opined that a big leaguer has to have determination in order to attain success. Further, he philosophized that for a person to gain respect and admiration one should also be tenacious. Observers feel that by any measure both Barry and Joe qualify as men of success, respect, and tenacity.

Barry concluded that his rise to, and success in, the major leagues fulfilled a lifetime dream, making his playing days the best days of his life. It's a good guess Dad feels the same way, too.

John McDonald

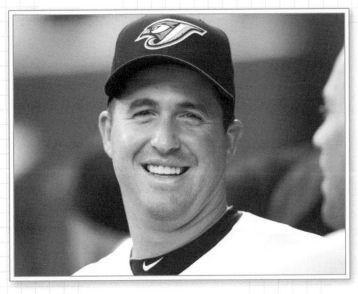

Photo Courtesy of Toronto Blue Jays

In one respect John McDonald has something in common with a current and a future Hall of Famer. Philadelphia Phillies pitcher Jim Bunning, Hall of Fame Class of '96, paid an unplanned tribute to his father on Father's Day in 1964 when he twirled a perfect game against the Mets. That gem gave him a no-hitter in both leagues and gave his father a terrific gift as well.

Ken Griffey, Jr. turned in a similar act of honoring his father when he tagged his 500th home run on Father's Day in 2004 with Senior on hand. After accepting the congratulations of his teammates near home plate, Junior, who had years earlier presented his father with the ball he hit for his 400th career homer (that one came on dad's fiftieth birthday), strolled over to the box his dad was sitting in and simply said, "Happy Father's Day."

Griffey, Sr. would later joke, "It was a nice Father's Day present, but it's an easy way to get out of giving me something. He used to do that for me for my birthday all the time." Remarkably, Junior's landmark homer that day marked the fourth time he had connected on a Father's Day and he had also thrown in eight more blasts on his father's birthday over his then sixteen-year career (he had also tossed in seven homers on Mother's Day). Interestingly, the Kid's 500th home run was also his 2,143rd lifetime hit, the same total his father had accumulated over his career. Meanwhile, Junior refuted his dad's comments about his presents saying he gave his father the same gift every Father's Day: "Old Spice and underwear," he grinned.

It's amazing how rich baseball lore is with so many coincidences and/or occasions in which a player arose to the occasion on a special day. Another moving and incredible story unfolded on Father's Day in 2010, a day not far removed from the death of McDonald's father. That year McDonald—a thirty-five-year-old Blue Jays infielder not known for the pop in his bat nor for popping off emotionally—hit his first home run of the season and just the fourteenth of his big league career which spread out over 1,900+ plate appearances, doing it for Dad. Not quite a Ruthian "called shot," but pretty close.

There's an old baseball expression which describes such improbable events: "It's like trying to catch lightning in a bottle." Well, what McDonald did was more like trying to seize a microbe out of mid-air with a pair of tweezers. However, when one factors in the inspiration McDonald had, with his father as his baseball muse, maybe his dramatic home run wasn't all that unlikely.

As John circled the bases he told himself he had to calm his emotions down. When he reached home plate, he briefly gave into those emotions, doing something which, for him, was quite atypical. John pointed to the sky, dedicating the hit to his father Jack who had passed away at the age of sixty just six days earlier after battling liver and kidney cancer for eight months.

As he entered the dugout "he pumped his fist and headed up the dugout tunnel to deal with his emotions." A group of teammates streamed down from the clubhouse and hugged McDonald, sharing in the electrically charged, goose bump-inducing moment.

Unlike some sons who lose their fathers suddenly, John knew his father was slipping away. He had known since March when doctors told Jack that his liver cancer, which had first been diagnosed the previous November, had recurred. Later on, knowing roughly how much time Jack had left, John made it a point to spend as much time with his father as possible. As a matter of fact, thanks to an understanding Blue Jays front office, John was away from his club during the final eleven days of Jack's life.

The last night of Jack's life was John's final chance, as he put it, to extend "our friendship further. His last night before he came home to hospice care, I stayed in the hospital with him all night and we sat up and we talked and we watched the sun come up. He would fall asleep and wake up an hour later and we would talk some more and they'd get more medication and we'd talk some more."

He continued, "That was a great night for both of us, because we knew what was going to happen the next day when we went home. He knew what direction it was going and so did I. It was a special night for the two of us. I said, 'Dad, I wish I had something to tell you that I never told you, but you know everything.'"

The final days of Jack's life were full of tears but, given the strength and love of these two men, also with laughter. As sports columnist Richard Griffin put it, they were "always celebrating a life well lived." That included an anecdote John shared: "One year I struck out only once in high school. We had a game where no umpire showed. They knew my dad was an ump so they pulled him out of the crowd. On a two-strike pitch, he punched me out on a curveball. We were talking in the hospital with a bunch of his umpire friends. I said, 'Dad, was that really a strike?' He said, 'Son, it was a strike then and it's a strike now.'"

John also revealed that earlier Jack had told him "that when I hit my next home run to point to him when I crossed home plate," said McDonald. "I told him, 'Dad, that may take awhile.' In the back of my mind I'm thinking I may have to play softball after I'm done playing baseball to do it, but I told him I would." He fulfilled his promise, coincidentally, on the day all sons celebrate their fathers. Furthermore, he had scant opportunity to cash in on the vow that day. He was not in the starting lineup and only entered the game as a substitute second baseman. He shook off the rust of inactivity—his last appearance in a game had taken place nearly a month earlier on May 23—and connected in the final inning for a two-run homer in his only at bat of the day.

"All I wanted to do was hit the ball hard. It was so bittersweet circling the bases," he articulated. "Whenever I've done something good on the baseball field, I'd call my mom and dad. It was an instant realization that he was gone. This is the first one I can't call home about."

McDonald also revealed that he would not even have been in the lineup so soon after his father's burial (two days earlier) except for his desire to honor his father and to live up to another promise he had made to him.

Over the last days of Jack's life, he and his son had many discussions. One pertained to a project the two of them had going, a father-son tradition which began back in John's days with the Cleveland Indians (from 1999 through 2004). "My dad and I had done a write-in contest online on why you want to bring your dad to the ballpark on Father's Day," John said. "We hosted twenty-five kids and their dads. And dad said to me, 'Make sure you're back in Toronto for Father's Day to honor this event because these kids are going to be waiting to see you.'" Originally, the two had planned for this to be their last opportunity to get together in Toronto to host the families, but when it became apparent Jack would

not be there, he insisted his son carry on. Clearly, John disappointed neither his fans nor his father.

The old expression, "Daddy didn't raise no fools" certainly applies to McDonald, an infielder capable of gliding to his left or right as smoothly and as effortlessly as a Zamboni machine. He always knew it was wise to listen to dad and, as a major leaguer, he continued the concept of soaking up the wisdom of his elders. That especially held true when he was with the Indians, a team which featured perennial Gold Glove winners Omar Vizquel at shortstop and Robby Alomar (the first son of a big leaguer to become a Hall of Famer) at second. McDonald said he picked their brains with buzzard-like eagerness, learning both technique and intangibles. McDonald revealed, "[Vizquel] taught me a little bit about being fearless, about how you have to know your limitations, you have to know your strengths." He learned well.

It's said that Willie Mays' glove is where triples went to die. McDonald's mitt is where sure-thing base hits meet their surprise demise. Many believe that if McDonald played on an everyday basis he would have won at least one Gold Glove. His lifetime fielding percentage at shortstop stands right around .970 and at second base it's pushing .990, better than Alomar's .984.

In Harmon Killebrew's Hall of Fame induction speech he credited his father, Harmon, Sr., who was a fine athlete, for giving him his first glove when he was eight years old, and for launching his career. When Harmon and his brother Bob tore up the front yard by playing countless ball games his mother would gripe that her sons were ruining the grass. "And my father," recalled Harmon, "would say, 'We're not raising grass here, we're raising boys.'" Like so many men who have lost their fathers, Harmon commented that he wished his father were still alive to share in the glory. He added that "somehow I know he is [here today]. Believe me, I know he is."

So, as McDonald gestured up to the skies upon touching home plate after his dramatic Father's Day homer he must have felt, just as Killebrew did, that his father is still with him, gazing down from above, proud of the boy that he loved so dearly.

Epilogue

A s I read John McDonald's story, misty-eyed, I could relate on a smaller scale to his sadness and to his pride. In July of 2002, almost exactly twenty-five years after my father had passed away, as a part of my promotional work for my book *Fathers, Sons, and Baseball*, I returned to my hometown in Pennsylvania to give a talk at the Donora Historical Society. Baseball has always been a big part not only of the Stewart family, but my hometown as well. I focused my presentation on Stan Musial and the two Griffeys, feeling that the Donora audience would appreciate hearing about their most famous native sons. Of all the talks I've given to groups, this one was by far the most enjoyable and rewarding. First of all, it was a great experience being embraced by my hometown—it was touching to see banners, flyers, and other signs welcoming me back home.

Receiving applause from my fellow Donorans felt strange though; one member of the audience had once been my homeroom teacher who nailed me for skipping school. That resulted in my getting swatted by our disciplinarian, a football coach who packed a mean wallop and left behind a large welt, a red badge of agony. Now my former homeroom teacher was actually applauding me—how incongruous, I thought. Here were folks who once thought of me as a mere kid (which, of course, I was), now asking for an autograph or asking me to pose with them for a picture. It was flattering and gratifying. I also felt vindicated. I felt like saying, "Hey, I skipped a little school (ironic because I wound up making a living teaching) and maybe I gave some teachers minor trouble, but I turned out all right."

I felt that somehow my father could see me that day. I felt as if he was smiling with a sense of pride in his only son.

How rewarding and touching it was to hear one woman say, "I knew your father. He was a sweet man." Another woman approached me to say, "Everybody loved O. J. [which stood for Owen Jesse]." While others had told me words to that effect before, I never tire of hearing such sentiments. Plus, they were correct: He was a wonderful man. Later, an elderly gentleman sidled up next to me as I autographed copies of my book and said, "I was O.J.'s neighbor and I have a picture of him I want you to have." What a rare prize, that picture. There stood my father at about the age of twenty-six, standing trim and strong in his U.S. Army uniform.

Still, not all of the pleasure of standing in front of the group was due to my father; a great deal had to do with my son, Scott (my other son, Sean, couldn't attend the event). Several times during my talk I glanced over at Scott, especially when I was discussing the love of fathers and sons. When it came time to introduce Scott, I proudly mentioned how he was infinitely more talented in baseball than I ever was, telling of his hitting exploits and of our hours spent together, bonded by baseball.

After the crowd filtered out of the building, Scott and I gathered up my display of books and strolled towards our car. "That was a good speech, Dad," he said. "A real good speech." Those few words made me feel happier than the applause I received and the overall glow of that unforgettable day combined. My day was truly complete.

The occasion had been similarly satisfying to my first-ever book signing that kicked off the sales of a book I wrote in 2001. That day, the presence of both of my sons enriched the event immeasurably. It was an event that simply *had* to be shared with them—without them the day would have felt hollow, so I was naturally proud and delighted to have them on hand along with my wife Nancy.

Now a third generation of Stewarts are playing baseball as my grandson, Sean's little boy Nathan, began his town's version of T-ball in the summer of 2011 at the age of four. Before his Manatees first practice, a set of rules for Blast Ball was passed out to each player. Rules? Rules for ballplayers three and four years old?! In reality we quickly learned there was only one rule in place: There are *no* rules.

Havoc quickly ensued from the very first contest. One boy reached first base, then picked it up and headed toward center field with it. Another took a pylon from behind home plate and placed it atop his cap, becoming an instant Conehead. All the chaos didn't really matter much—the exposure to baseball was a start for Nathan. After all, many such legions of young boys, some future big leaguers, have such humble roots in the game.

I envision the future with Sean and Nathan spending a slew of hours together involved in the sport—be it playing catch, talking baseball, or watching games from sofa seats, to crude bleacher perches at youth league games, to box seats in big league parks. The bond they form as well will last long after I'm gone. That is the nature of baseball and of father-son love.

And so the baton is passed on and on and on.

About the Author

Wayne Stewart was born and raised in Donora, Pennsylvania, a town that has produced several big league baseball players, including Stan Musial and the father-son Griffeys. Stewart now lives in Lorain, Ohio, with his wife, Nancy. They have two sons, Sean and Scott, and one grandson, Nathan.

Wayne has covered the sports world as a writer for more than thirty years, beginning in 1978. He has interviewed and profiled many stars including Nolan Ryan, Bob Gibson, Tony Gwynn, Greg Maddux, Rickey

Henderson, and Ken Griffey, Jr. and has written biographies of Babe Ruth, Alex Rodriguez, and Musial.

In addition, he has written twenty-five baseball books, a book on the subject of football, and one book on basketball. His works have also appeared in seven baseball anthologies.

He has also written more than 500 articles for publications such as *Baseball Digest, USA Today/Baseball Weekly, Boys' Life,* and *Beckett Publications.*

He has written for many major league official team publications such as the Braves, Yankees, White Sox, Orioles, Padres, Twins, Phillies, Red Sox, A's, and Dodgers.

Furthermore, Stewart has appeared, as a baseball expert/historian, on Cleveland's Fox 8 and on an ESPN Classic television show. He also hosted his own radio shows including a call-in sports talk show, a pre-game Indians report, and pre-game shows for Notre Dame football.

Sources

Brantley Chapter

Assenheimer, Chris. "Rising Star." *The Chronicle-Telegram.*

Author's interviews with Michael Brantley.

Hoynes, Paul. "Five Questions With . . . Indians Left Fielder Michael Brantley." *The Plain Dealer.*

Milicia, Joe. "Tribe Nets Brantley in CC Trade." *Associated Press* item.

Chamberlain Chapter

http://newsandsentinel.com/page/content.detail/id/139575/Yankees-RHP-Chamberlain-has-torn-elbow-ligament-.html?isap=1&nav=5076

http://sports.yahoo.com/mlb/blog/big_league_stew/post/World-Series-moment-Joba Chamberlain-and-his-da?urn=mlb-200353

Smith, Gary. "What's Love Got to Do With It." *Sports Illustrated.*

Drew Chapter

Author's interview with J. D. Drew.

http://www.chattanoogan.com/articles/article_47264.asp

Duncan Chapter

Author's interview with Shelley Duncan.

Dulik, Brian. "Regular Playing Time Suits Duncan Just Fine." *The Chronicle-Telegram*.

Hoynes, Paul. "Father and Son." *The Plain Dealer*.

———. "It Appears Cabrera is Running Out of Gas." *The Plain Dealer*.

———. "Five Questions With . . . Indians Outfielder/Infielder Shelley Duncan." *The Plain Dealer*.

Lubinger, Bill. "Indian or Clipper, Duncan Stays Ready." *The Plain Dealer*.

"Spring Gives Big Unit Chance vs. Lefties." *USA Today Sports Weekly*.

Winston, Lisa. "NL Central Prospects: St. Louis Cardinals." *USA Today Sports Weekly*.

Francoeur Chapter

Author's interviews with Jeff Francoeur.

http://www.jockbio.com/Bios/Franc/Franc_bio.html

Garvey Chapter

Author's interview with Darol Salazar.

Email to author from Garvey.

Garvey, Steve. *My Bat Boy Days*.

http://articles.latimes.com/2011/may/19/sports/la-sp-0520-sondheimer-column-20110520

http://philadelphia.cbslocal.com/2011/06/07/will-ryan-garvey-be-around-for-phils-in-june-draft/

Gonzalez (Luis) Chapter

Author's interview with Luis Gonzalez.

Callahan, Gerry. "Mr. Generosity." *Sports Illustrated*.

Click, Paul. "Arizona's Luis Gonzalez Finds Late Success Rewarding." *Baseball Digest*.

Habib, Daniel G. "It's Good To Be Gonzo." *Sports Illustrated* Special
    Issue.
Nightengale, Bob. "Late Bloomer." *USA Today Baseball Weekly.*

Gonzalez (Adrian) Chapter
Author's interview with Adrian Gonzalez.
Benjamin, Amalie. "Baseball A Way of Life For Adrian Gonzalez."
    Baseball Digest.
http://www.agonzalez23.com/eng/bios.html
Krasovic, Tom. "Padres' Adrian Gonzalez: First Class at First Base."
    Baseball Digest.

Hamilton Chapter
Author's interview with Tom Grieve.
Hamilton, Josh with Tim Keown. *Beyond Belief.*
Savage, Ted. *Josh Hamilton.*

Jones Chapter
Author's interviews with Chipper Jones.
Glavine, Tom, Larry Jones Sr., et al. *Chipper Jones: A Brave Legend in the
    Making.*
Zack, Bill. *Chipper Jones.*
http://www.ajc.com/sports/atlanta-braves/chipper-is-always-
    dads-553397.html
http://bats.blogs.nytimes.com/2009/06/24/chipper-jones-gets-seats-
    from-shea-stadium/
http://content.usatoday.com/communities/dailypitch/
    post/2010/06/chipper-jones-retire/1
http://mlb.mlb.com/news/article.jsp?ymd=20110506&content_
    id=18709950&vkey=news_atl&c_id=atl&partnerId=rss_atl
http://sportsillustrated.cnn.com/2008/writers/michael_
    bamberger/06/10/jones0616/index.html#ixzz1QmnUJdjb

http://www.outsidethebeltway.com/chipper_jones_names_son_after_shea_stadium/

LaRoche Chapter

Author's interview with Adam LaRoche.

Biertempfel, Ron. "In the Swing of Things." *Pittsburgh Tribune-Review*.

"Bucs Brothers." *USA Today*.

Livingstone, Seth. "Q & A With Adam LaRoche: First Baseman Has Confidence in his — and Braves' — Abilities." *USA Today Sports Weekly*.

Newberry, Paul. "Bad Play Brings Light to LaRoche's ADD." *The Plain Dealer*.

McDonald Chapter

Author's interview with John McDonald.

Hoynes, Paul. "McDonald's Rare Homer a Special One." *The Plain Dealer*.

http://www.thestar.com/sports/baseball/mlb/bluejays/article/826240—griffin-for-the-jays-john-mcdonald-an-especially-poignant-father-s-day?bn=1

Perez Chapter

Hoynes, Paul. "Five Questions With . . . Indians Closer Chris Perez." *The Plain Dealer*.

Lubinger, Bill. "Perez Closes With Hair and Flair." *The Plain Dealer*.

Nightengale, Bob. "Indians Bang a Winning Drum." *USA Today Sports Weekly*.

http://bleacherreport.com/articles/618645-2011-mlb-exclusive-interview-cleveland-indians-chris-pure-rage-perez by Alan Harrison.

http://sportsillustrated.cnn.com/2011/writers/mel_antonen/05/06/paternity.leave/index.html

www.cleveland.com/tribe/index.ssf/2011/04/five_questions_with_
 indians_cl.html

www.imgacademies.com/baseball-academy/news/father-of-all-star-
 chris-perez-proudly-sports-a-stellar-ring/1211/

Reflections on Fathers and Sons

Assenheimer, Chris. "Byrd Just Wants Respect." *The Chronicle-Telegram.*

Associated Press, "Snow's Father Proud of Son's Big Day." *The Morning Journal.*

Blum, Ronald. "Local Boy Stings Angels." *The Chronicle-Telegram.*

Dow, Bill. "Remembering Sparky Anderson And the Secret of His Success." *Baseball Digest.*

Ginsburg, David. "Ripken's Son Filling Big Shoes." *The Chronicle-Telegram.*

Hoynes, Paul. "Teammates Pass the Cap for Tribe's Hannahan." *The Plain Dealer.*

_____. "Indians Chatter." *The Plain Dealer.*

"Inner Game: Mets Outfielder Tony Tarasco." *Sports Illustrated.*

Jaynes, Roger. *Al McGuire: The Colorful Warrior.*

Livingstone, Seth and Howard Balzer. "Memorializing Munson." *USA Today Sports Weekly.*

Manoloff, Dennis. "Indians Great Thome Driven by Practice, Respect and Pride." *The Plain Dealer.*

Pluto, Terry. "A Grateful Heart Fuels Thome's Bat." *The Plain Dealer.*

Robinson, Alan. "Jim Leyland Happily Returns to Coaching—in Youth League." *The Valley Independent.*

Stewart, Wayne. *Fathers, Sons, and Baseball.*

"The Blotter." *Sports Illustrated.*

Waszak, Jr., Dennis. "3 Managers' Sons Among Draftees." *The Chronicle-Telegram.*

Wire service reports. "Williams Might Have to Leave Yankees Again." *The Chronicle-Telegram* (May 11, 2001).

www.fathersandfamilies.org/?tag=john-franco

http://nbcsports.msnbc.com/id/31467672/ns/sports-baseball/

http://reds.enquirer.com/2000/10/26/red_sullivan_john_franco.html

http://sportsillustrated.cnn.com/baseball/mlb/1999/postseason
    world_series/news/1999/10/27/oneill_plays_ap/

www.luistiant.com/biography/

www.tcpalm.com/news/2011/sep/08/family-reunion/

The Tim McCarver Show

Sabathia Chapter

Author's interview with CC Sabathia.

Hoynes, Paul. "All-Star Notebook." *The Plain Dealer*.

http://sports.espn.go.com/espnmag/story?id=3310783

Shea, Therese. *CC Sabathia*.

Withers, Tom. "C.C. Sabathia Fulfills a Dream." *The Chronicle-Telegram*.

www.usatoday.com/sports/baseball/al/yankees/2010-10-14-cc-
    sabathia-new-york-yankees-pitcher-postseason_N.htm

Zito Chapter

Albee, Dave. "The BIG One." *Sporting News*.

"Commiserate Comebacks." *USA Today*.

Reiter, Ben. "Dangerous Curve." *Sports Illustrated*.

Silver, Michael. "Inside the Head of Barry Zito." *Sports Illustrated*.

Sorci, Rick. "Baseball Profile Barry Zito—Oakland A's." *Baseball Digest*.

"We Will Rock You." *Sports Illustrated*.

Note: additional quotes on Williams and his father from wire report
    stories in *The Morning Journal* and *The Plain Dealer*